Charlestown to Charlestown and Beyond

Mike Nolan

Clink Street

London | New York

I would like to dedicate this book to the memory of two very beautiful and exceptional people, Alexander and Sascha Pincowski. They had the terrible misfortune to be in the very close proximity of a suicide bomber who detonated his device while they stood at the check-in desk of American Airlines at Brussels Airport on March 22nd 2016, killing them both instantly along with fourteen others. The bomber's actions not only took these lives but also devastated the lives of Alexander and Sascha's parents, Ed & Marjan, their families and friends, as well as depriving the world of the opportunity to watch this special brother and sister achieve their hopes and dreams, and to reach the great heights that they where destined to.

I would also like to pay my respects to Merrete Bruel on the very sad loss of her husband Christian. I will always remember his kindness.

Preface

It was a warm, balmy evening as we had just watched a dazzlingly beautiful sunset, the bright crimson globe had just dipped below the horizon, as the last haze of daylight surrendered to the night, it became dark almost instantly, as there is very little twilight in the Caribbean, we were en route to St Maarten, having left the anchorage at Guadeloupe in the Caribbean Sea.

Our ship, *Hafan-Y-Mor*, was an 85 ft LOA Brigantine Schooner. She was our home, as well as providing us with an income, she was the end result of many years of blood, sweat, and tears. All of the sacrifices and effort that we had put into this project was now being repaid in spades. All our hopes and aspirations had come to fruition, and the dream that had been mine for many years was now being shared with Viv. Our future prospects were looking more positive after a couple of successful charters, we were living the dream.

We were running the ship with a crew of four on this particular passage, this was fine for short island hopping. Viv and myself were accompanied by Molino, a South American sailor on his way to St Maarten, along with Magnus a young Swede; these guys were working and paying for their passage.

All was well after completing my evening rounds. Magnus and I went below, Molino was on the helm, he spotted a red light, he called me, I came up on deck to take a look, using the trusted, mark one eyeball and a hand-bearing compass. I was sure that this was the island of Nevis. I went below to the Nav station, checked the chart, and the Satnav confirmed it was Nevis. The chart stated that an all round red light signalled that it was the harbour at Charlestown, we were about two miles distant. I told Molino to keep the light on his starboard side, visible between the mainmast and the shrouds. I returned to our cabin. Suddenly, I heard, and felt, a sickening grinding crunch as the ship lost all forward movement and it stopped. I quickly scrambled up the companionway out on to the deck. I looked puzzlingly at the strange angle of the rigging. My mind would not register the severe degree of the list of the deck. Somehow Molino had driven the ship onto the reef. Instinctively, I knew that the dream had been well and truly shattered, and that it had turned into my worst nightmare.

I was born in Birkenhead just after the end of the Second World War. Home was a condemned, three-storey Victorian terrace, with no electricity, but we did have the luxury of an outside WC. This house was rented by an elderly widower, Tom Cairns, due to his kindness, or it may have been pity, he allowed my mother to sublet a couple of the rooms. I lived with my mother, her name was Mary. I had two brothers and a sister, John was the eldest brother, I was next in line just ahead of Thomas, our sister Valerie completed the line-up. As a single parent my mother worked tirelessly to keep her children fed and clothed, she always had two or three jobs on the go all at the same the time and I will be eternally grateful for the work ethic that she instilled into us as children. We did not have a lot, but we did not go cold or hungry, and we were all able to achieve a high degree of independence.

I have very distinctive memories of receiving my first book, it was a Christmas present from my Aunty Betty. She was our posh relative, she lived in Pensby on the Wirral, with my Uncle John, they had two children, John and Carol.

As well as being my first proper book, it was also the first book that I had read from cover to cover. The book was *Treasure Island* by Robert Louis Stevenson, to imply that it made an impression on me would be a classic understatement, I was totally immersed, I became Jim Hawkins, and I was convinced that given the opportunity I would opt for 'Piracy' as my career of choice.

My childhood memories are all very good, bearing in mind that we were all part of a dysfunctional family long before it achieved the fashionable status that it holds today.

My playground existed entirely in my imagination; in real life, we were surrounded by the remains of shops and houses that had the misfortune of being on the flight path that the German Luftwaffe followed when they were trying to obliterate the shipyards, and the docks that sat along the waterfront of the River Mersey.

Many of the buildings that had been bombed were transformed in to castles, and mountains. Many of these buildings had subterranean cellars that masquerade as grottos and smugglers' caves. We were so blessed, that there was no such thing as Elf & Safety when I was growing up.

When we needed more of a challenge, after reaching the summit of what we called Everest repeatedly, the novelty soon wore thin. For a little more adventure we would then head down to the docks. Now this presented an altogether different approach, there was always the Dock Gate Bobby on the lookout, along with the occasional watchman that we had to avoid, but we soon found many ways to bypass what passed as security, we must have been invisible to the watchers. Given all the choices that we had, both the Bidston and the Vittoria dock were our favourite's, with the Bidston being the absolute favourite, this was mainly due to the close proximity of the Mersey rail line, this was a tried and tested escape route when we got chased by the dock police, which was quite often, once we were off the dock property, the Mersey rail police took over.

In reality the waters were full of whatever pollutants that were swilling around in the bilges of many of the cargo ships, and tramp steamers that used the port facilities when they were emptying their bilges as they laid alongside, by pumping it all overboard. Yes the waters were cold, dirty and full of slimy garbage, but to me it was a lush tranquil paradise, the cranes and derricks took on the appearance of swaying palms that were festooned with masses of coconuts that lined the water's edge. The splintered remains of an old ship's lifeboat had been transformed into the Hispaniola. This was an ideal training ground for perfecting and honing the very essential survival skills that would be put to good use in the pristine sparkling azure warm – but just as unforgiving – waters of the Eastern Caribbean Sea some 45 years later.

I would like to dedicate this book to the memory of two beautiful souls that had the terrible misfortune to be in the very close proximity of a deranged suicide bomber on that fateful day of the 22nd March 2016, at the American Airline's check-in desk at Brussels airport. His misguided actions not only took the lives of these two children, Alexander and Sacha, it also devastated the lives of their parents, Ed and Marjan, their families and friends, as well as depriving the world of the opportunity to watch these two special people achieve their dreams, hopes, and to aspire to the heights that they were destined to achieve.

The children's names are Alexander & Sascha Pinczowski. Their parents are Ed & Marjan.

My lady (friend) Vivien and I left the Wirral to setup a new home together, after falling hopelessly in love over a bowl of cornflakes, no, this was no romantic breakfast, we had been working together in a factory that produced breakfast cereals.

We headed south and ended up in Exeter. I was a part-time musician so I had arranged a meeting with a fellow musician who was looking for a drummer. His name was Trevor, he owned a large Victorian house, and he used the upper floors as self-contained student lets; he very graciously gave us an empty bedsit until we could find our feet.

We soon found a job with accommodation provided, all we had to do was look after the needs of an elderly lady and her dogs. It was a big old mansion house in a village called Spreyton, just a couple of miles outside Crediton. Viv was a dog person, she liked the idea of helping the old lady with her dogs, but she wanted a dog of her own, this idea did not go down too well with me, I was not too keen on having a pet. I relented, and we went along to the local rescue centre and we came away with a puppy, it was a crossbred Labrador/Red Setter, it was a female, so I called her 'Fluke', because she looked like the picture on the cover of a book that I had read by James Herbert. The dog decided that I was its master, she was quite well-behaved when she could see you, out of sight out of mind! She was very dizzy, we once made the mistake of leaving her in the car with a box of groceries, what she didn't eat, she totally wrecked!!

Viv was able to find a job in a factory in Okehampton, the only downside was that it involved a 22 mile round-trip, twice a day. One of Viv's colleagues suggested that she got a moped. We went along to the dealer, and he suggested rather than a moped a 125cc motorcycle would be better. He delivered it a couple of days later, we bought a set of 'L' plates, and let Viv loose on the unsuspecting motorists of Devon. In all fairness she's done very well; she only had one minor mishap when she actually fell off it, whereas I was forever falling off the bloody infernal machine.

Eventually we found a nice little cottage to rent in the village of Folly Gate, it was only a couple of minutes away from Viv's workplace, needless to say significantly reducing her travelling time.

My brother Thomas and his wife Marlene decided to head south as well, they rented a mobile home on a residential site in Okehampton.

Not long after we settled in, the Welsh contingent started to come visiting. Viv's brother-in-law, Bob, and Sue his wife were the first, they had a good time. Viv's parents, Tom and Megan were next on the list, we drove up to Wales, picked them up and returned the following day. During their visit I had arranged for us all to attend a concert in Torquay. Coincidently, the show clashed with Viv's birthday, both Tom Megan, and Viv thought that this was the birthday treat. Unbeknown to her, I had arranged a surprise party. Thomas, Marlene, plus a couple of Viv's workmates were waiting just round the corner of our drive, as we drove out, they drove in. They done a brilliant job decorating the room, as well as preparing a fabulous buffet. As it was a late afternoon show, nobody had eaten, when we left the theatre both Tom and Megan, suggested that we find a local restaurant go for a drink and something to eat, I refused, saying that I would not drink and drive. A few miles further on Megan then insisted that we stop for fish and chips, once again I had an excuse not to stop, as she glared at me, I could see the bemused look of puzzlement on her face. She told me that she was starving, and Tom could do with a pint, even Viv was getting a wee bit tetchy. As we got to the top of our drive, I could see that all the cars had been hidden out of sight, and that the house was in darkness. I opened the front door, let Tom, Megan, and Viv in to the living room, all the lights came on, and a rousing shout of 'SURPRISE SURPRISE, Happy Birthday'. The commotion frightened the life out of Megan, she flew out of the door then upstairs to her room to get over the shock. She was eventually enticed down by the wonderful aroma of the hot buffet. Viv was mightily relieved, she thought that she had discovered my dark side.

I found a job doing some labouring work on a farm, the owner was a Mr Ian Peters, he was a tree surgeon, as well is a very accomplished climber, I ended up spending more time working with him rather than on the farm. I met a couple of guys from Crediton, they were looking for a drummer, but they were all into heavy rock, this was not really my type of music. I rehearsed with them over a couple of months, even got as far as playing a few live gigs with them. This band was called 'Fluke', the lead singer was called George, he must have been a fan of James Herbert books.

Things were going very well for both of us. We decided to buy a mobile home on the same residential site in Okehampton where Thomas and Marlene were living. Once we settled in we started to receive more visits from Viv's family.

Viv and I decided to get married, and we would have the reception at the White Hart Hotel. The manager was an ex-Mancunian, his name was Tony. He very kindly gave us the venue, including the bridal suite, Thomas and Marlene provided and prepared the food, then all of my newfound musician friends provided the entertainment. We had four different bands, it was a musical extravaganza. All of Vivien's family, except her brother Kevin, made the journey down to Okehampton for the wedding. Kevin's wife Christine, had only just recently given birth to their first daughter Sarah, so a long road trip was out of the question.

The guy I was working for, Ian, and his partner Maggie, very kindly offered their farm for the accommodation of Viv's family. Everybody had a really good weekend and it culminated with a fantastic Sunday lunch in the restaurant for all our family and close friends – that was some wedding feast, a proper three-day event.

Viv started work as a carer at a council-run care home in Okehampton, The husband of one of her colleagues was putting a dance band together and he needed a drummer, I went along for a chat and got the job. This was a ten-piece dance band with a brass section. The rehearsals were a little bit tedious so the rhythm section, which consisted of Nick Worsley the vocalist, three guitarists, and myself, usually ended up, out of sheer boredom, playing as a five-piece band, while we were waiting for the brass section to agree on what particular song they wanted to do, as well as endeavouring find a key that they all could play in. We had a couple of gigs as the big band, then one night during the interval we played as a five-piece band, it went down very well, so, by mutual agreement, we decided to quit from the big band then went on to perform as a five-piece, the band was called 'Cloud'. We were getting plenty of work travelling as far as Falmouth in the south and Dorset in the east. I had bought a battered old Ford Capri to use as a runabout, it got me to and from work, as Viv was working full-time, therefore the dog had to come with me. This was not an issue if we were working off the farm, she would just jump on the back of a Land Rover and she would always come with us. There was a shed in the garden she used to sleep in, when we were home during the day at the weekend she would be tied up in the garden. One sunny day the local sheepdog came along and she ended up very pregnant. Sue and her husband Bob came down for the weekend, the band had a gig in Barnstable on the Saturday night, all four of us were having lunch in the beer garden of the Fountain Inn, the dog was very agitated sitting under the table. They decided to take the dog back home, she just about made it to the shed when the first puppy arrived, we got home about an hour later the puppy count was five. Viv decided that she would not be coming out with us to the gig she wanted to stay home and keep an eye on 'Fluke', we left at about six o'clock, the count had gone up to seven. we arrived at the gig, got set up, and done the first set, Viv had the number of the venue, so she called twice, when she made the second call I was actually playing so the MC interrupted the performance to announce that the drummer had just become a dad to nine pups. On the Monday morning Ian Peters came to pick me up for work in his Land Rover, so I left my car in the parking lot. When Vivien came home from work she was greeted by a couple of irate neighbours, they were concerned about the well-being of the litter of pups – somehow 'Fluke' had managed to chew her way out of the shed, completely abandoning her pups. She climbed onto the bonnet of my car and howled incessantly, she was still howling when I came home, only then would she go back in to the shed to look after the puppies. The following day I had to put the dog basket, the pups, and 'Fluke' on the back seat of the car, that was the only way I could leave. I felt like Noah. This worked well for about two weeks, as the puppies got bigger, so did their poopsies. They would climb all over the inside of the car, when I came to a set of traffic lights it was impossible to drive off until I had managed to fish any stray pups out of the foot well. I could not use the foot pedals. Fellow motorists often gave me very puzzling, strange looks, all they could see was the driver's head disappearing into the foot well and coming up then throwing puppies over his shoulder into the back seat. The aroma in the car left a lot to be desired as well. Fortunately as they grew older Viv was able to find homes for them all, then we took 'Fluke' to the vet to make sure it didn't happen again. When the pups had all gone, the Ford Capri had to go as well. The night before it went I poured a bottle of bleach into the boot and the foot wells, then I just drove it to the breaker's yard and handed over the keys.

Viv's sister, Avril, came for a visit, she liked it so much she ended up staying with us for a wee while! Then she eventually found a job and an apartment in Exeter. Shortly afterwards, Nerys, their youngest sister moved down from Ruthin to move into the apartment with Avril. It was beginning to look like that we had started a mini Welsh migration. We needed another car, as we were likely to be making frequent visits to North Wales we opted for a decent car, the chosen one was a Ford Granada GL.

2

One of the venues my band played at quite often was the Okehampton Motel. I became friendly with the manager. His name was Dennis. It was not unusual for all four of us at one time or another to end up working either behind the bar or in the kitchen. I can remember one particular show that we put on featured an 'exotic dancer' no, not a stripper, she was a 'belly dancer' part of her act featured her dancing with an immensely great snake, that was fine until she brought the snake to the tables. My brother Thomas was terrified of the snake; for a long time it was the subject of much amusement for all of us. Dennis and Avril became an item, they eventually got married.

Things were looking quite rosy for us when we found ourselves in the position of being able to afford the luxury of buying our first home together. The house was very primitive with no bathroom and an outside toilet, we completely renovated it, starting at the top with a new roof, and everything else underneath it.

My eldest son Christopher, had just joined the Royal Navy. All new recruits do their basic training at HMS Raleigh in Torpoint, just a few miles from Plymouth. I can't recall how the meeting was brokered, but he wanted to meet with me. We had a meaningful chat and when we parted he said, 'That we should do it again.' The next time I met him he came home with me to meet with Viv. The relationship blossomed, he even brought a couple of his mates to one of our gigs.

I was going to do some work for Ian Peters. I was driving towards Mill farm it was a very narrow typical country lane. Just up ahead there was a Y-junction. I needed to go off to the left at this junction, this is where the school bus collected the schoolchildren. As there was no footpath I was always weary as I came up to this bend. Suddenly there was a loud crash and my windscreen shattered. When I got out of the car there were the remnants of a motorcycle jammed under the nearside of my car. Approximately 15 feet behind the car a motorcyclist was lying in the road, and he appeared to badly hurt, he was in a bad way. I called the emergency services, and an ambulance and a police car arrived pretty quickly. The young man was taken to hospital in Exeter. The traffic officer checked the car and the road surface, took all the necessary measurements and arranged for the car and the motorcycle to be removed to their compound. As I was a little shook up he advised me to come into the station the next day to make a statement. By the time that I arrived at Mill Farm the whole community were aware that there had been an accident and that I had been involved. Ian told me that they had just heard the young man on the motorcycle was the son of one of the neighbouring farmers, and that he was in a critical condition. His name was Joe, and he used to do some part-time gardening for Ian's mother, and he was in a critical condition. I was a bit shook-up so Ian drove me back home. Viv and I went to the police station the next day to make a statement. I couldn't recall anything different from what I told the policeman on the day before, I did not see the motorbike , it seemed to be going very fast when he came round the bend, I couldn't avoid him, he hit me. The policeman confirmed that my nearside wheel was nine inches from the bottom of the hedgerow, the motorcycle struck the centre of car. The motorcyclist was on the wrong side of the road, travelling at speed, the accident was unavoidable. The policeman asked me 'if I wanted to pursue a prosecution.' I declined, I thought that he would be paying enough of a price, the motorcycle was a write-off, and he was going to be hospitalised for quite a while. The policeman also advised me that my car was a write-off, and asked me again 'are sure you don't want to seek a conviction?' I replied, 'No thanks the lad has had enough bad luck,' to which the policeman replied, 'You are the lucky one.' I replied, 'How come there's not a scratch on me?' I was advised that my car was in the compound and it was suggested that I should look at it and check the steering wheel. We were horrified at the extent of the damage to the front of the car; the steering wheel was buckled, apparently he had crashed through the windscreen and his head had hit the steering wheel and buckled it, his forward momentum had thrown him over the roof of the car. If he had been a little bit higher he would have missed the steering wheel and crushed my chest. I threw up a very violently.

It was on an early Sunday evening, were heading south from Exeter along the A30. We were heading home after a very enjoyable weekend playing sailors. Vivien and I, were the proud owners of a, 24 ft van-de-stadt, Buccaneer sloop. That we kept moored, on the River Exe at Topsham. Somehow I had managed to convince Viv that being a sailor was fun. She took to it very well considering the fact that she could not swim. We lived in Okehampton, in a house that we had just spent all the money we had on, and two hard years renovating it. We were just passing through Sticklepath when Vivien, in a moment of brevity, said, 'That was a great weekend, why don't we get a bigger boat then we can, just literally, sail off into the sunset?' This took me completely unaware – as well as not being able to swim, when you combine that with a tangible, but irrational fear of water, that does not lend itself to the prospects of an idyllic life on the ocean wave. It is a massive responsibility, when your dreams and aspirations conflict and impact on the life of the one person on the planet that you are predisposed to look after and protect with every fibre of your being for the rest of their life. All that any human being in this world can hope for is that this inequitable faith, trust, and hope for the future are not misguided or misplaced.

I must admit, that took me by surprise, my reply to that, was that 'a bigger boat will cost a lot of money.' She casually replied, 'Then why don't we sell the house?' Now, that did surprise me! 'Do you actually mean that we should just sell up and sail?' Bearing in mind that we had spent the last two years living in a building site, without all the modern amenities that we take for granted now, just basic things like a toilet, running water, central heating, and above all, a kitchen. When we got home, I put the kettle on and made a cup of tea, fed the cat and the dog, then we decided to talk about the house that we had worked long and hard to transform from the shell of a building into the beautiful home that we were both very proud of. To finance the whole renovation project, we both had two and sometimes three jobs on the go. Viv was working at a care home during the day, from there she would go to the egg packing factory, for a couple of hours of putting eggs into boxes, then she would nip home, get washed and changed, then go on to work behind the bar at the White Hart, that was our local watering hole.

I was also doing some work with Ian Peters, a local tree surgeon, and, I was also involved in the construction of the new, Okehampton bypass, if I found myself with some free time, I would also pack eggs ,and help out at the White Hart. My brother, Thomas was the chef there, he also worked with me on the bypass job, and on a few other, projects that we were involved in.

Thomas and his wife Marlene, lived in a chalet at the caravan park in Okehampton, where we would sit for hours going over our dreams and plans of exactly what we wanted to do. Bear in mind this was definitely a case of the blind leading the blind. We were not really sure of just exactly what we were going to do. The basic plan, was to find a boat big enough for the four of us to live on. I started to look in earnest, from the yachting mags, to MOD surplus auction sites. Travelling to London on two occasions to view prospective boats. I found a 48 ft plastic sailboat, without rigging, moored at Eel Pie Island, in Middlesex.

All four of us, and our dog Fluke, drove to Middlesex to check this boat out. It was moored on an island, we had to cross a footbridge to get to it, the dog was terrified of crossing water. Even when I tried to carry her she was still petrified, so much so, we had to leave the dog in the car. Obviously this is going to be a major problem, a dog that doesn't like water living on a boat. Fortunately, we were only going to spend one night on board, but that gave us a good idea of what we were letting ourselves in for. We were quite impressed with the boat, and the amount of room, bearing in mind this was now being used as a live aboard houseboat, and so it had never been rigged or sailed. We were all of the opinion that it fitted the bill, and with the right help, we could proceed. We eventually agreed a price with the owner, and agreed to sleep on it and sort out the final details when we get back to Devon. When we got home, after much deliberation, we decided that the logistics of fitting and rigging the boat where she was berthed, was untenable. We had already agreed a price then. Fortunately the owner called me to advise me that he had decided the boat was worth more to him as a houseboat, than to sell it to me as a boat, so our problem was solved for us, and the search resumed again in earnest.

3

One of my part-time jobs was driving a delivery van for a local laundry. This laundry had many contracts with the MOD that involved me making, deliveries and collections from Royal Naval shore establishments, and the naval dockyard in Plymouth.

I came across an ad in the local rag for a hull for sale, it was in Wadebridge. I found the location where the vessel was berthed, and on one of my trips out for the laundry I went to see it, it was love at first sight! I was smitten.

She was a ferrocement hull, leaning on her starboard side against the harbour wall on the River Camel at Wadebridge. She was 68 ft on deck, 17 ft beam, 10 1/2 ft draft. With the addition of the bowsprit and the bumpkin it gave her an overall length is just under 85 ft, with a gross weight of 60 tons. I could not wait to get home to spread the good news.

I called the owner – this gentleman was a hotelier from Trevone Bay, he agreed to meet me and discuss the boat. We met at Wadebridge and he gave me a brief outline of the ship's history. He told me that the boat had been a self-build project for a local couple who wanted to charter it. Unfortunately the couple had major financial problems, they decided, that for purely financial reasons they should get a divorce which would help them resolve some of their financial issues. Tragically, the wife passed away suddenly and as the boat was registered in her name, due to the divorce the husband had ceased to be the next of kin. This caused more problems than it solved, the boat was eventually sold to pay off some of the debts. It had been acquired by the gentleman from Trevone head, this was the gentleman that I bought it from.

I decided that I definitely needed to get suitable qualifications for sailing the ship. I enrolled at the local college to do night classes on a RYA course. I got my competent crew ticket, I then went for a five-day, practical, day skippers course. I passed that one, I then went on to do the ,'offshore skippers course'. I then enrolled for further night classes, for a celestial navigation course. On my way home from one of the night classes in Exeter, it was a filthy night, and I picked up a hitch-hiker, he was heading for Okehampton, I told him it was his lucky night. during the conversation, he told me that he was taking up a position in a factory in Okehampton as part of his engineering degree, and he would be looking for accommodation close to the town.

During the conversation I told them I'd been to Twickenham last week 'for the Rugby.' He said, 'I was there too,' I told him that I was there to look at a boat, and I told him of our plans. His reply was 'then you must have a house to sell.' I said, 'Yes' and proceeded to give him the full estate agent's spiel. He said, 'Yes I will buy it.'

I dropped him off at the White Hart, he said, 'Good night and thanks for the lift.' I didn't see him again for another couple of months.

We put the house on the market with local estate agent, because it had been very tastefully renovated we had a lot of interest, and a lot of nosy sightseers, one of whom, I personally threw out. I was very proud of my kitchen, I personally, had cut, and slabbed the elm trunk that was used.

Ian Peters, the tree surgeon I used to work for, had a son-in-law, his name was Peach, and he was a craftsman. He made me a bespoke, handmade kitchen, the cretin who came to view the house had the audacity to tell me that the first thing that they would do would be to rip the kitchen out – the viewing didn't last long. Then one afternoon I answered the doorbell to find a young man standing there. He was very annoyed, he told me that he had just seen the house advertised in the estate agents. I said, 'That is correct, the house is for sale.' Very indignantly he said to me that I had promised to sell it to him and it should not be in the estate agent's window, and in no uncertain terms he told me that I should remove it from there. 'But you haven't even seen it,' I said to him, 'how could you possibly buy something unseen?' His reply to that was, 'Did you describe it accurately?' 'Yes,' I said. 'And were you telling the truth?' 'Yes,' I said. 'Then that is good enough for me. Now you should take it off the market, consider it sold, do you want cash?'

Sitting here with my feet up, enjoying a nice Remy Martin, looking around at all the work that we've done, the penny finally drops, that we have just taken the first tentative steps of a very eventful journey, that once it has started, we will be powerless to find that the stop button that will put an end to this roller-coaster ride.

Due to the fact that we sold the house, complete with fixtures and fittings – and that means everything, from furniture, floor coverings, filled bookshelves, to brass ornaments and all the horse brasses that were decorating the fireplaces – the only things that I would be taking with me were Fluke, Tibbles and Viv, that is, the dog, the cat and the wife, not much baggage there then.

When Thomas, Marlene, Vivien, and the dog, came with me to Wadebridge to check the boat out, it became very clear that the dog would not voluntarily set foot on the boat, it just did not like crossing water.

Thomas, Marlene and Viv all had reservations; after some discussion, they agreed to go along with it in principle. firstly we have to find a home for the dog, as it would not be coming with us. Viv was not too pleased about that. We decided we would move onto the boat as long as we could get basic services. We made some good friends. There were two brothers that had a garage literally on the quay, they allowed us to hook up to their water and power supply, what more could we need?

We all agreed that Thomas, Marlene and Viv would seek employment and keep working full-time, leaving me to do most of the work on the boat,

We then went home, and started the proceedings of selling up and moving out. Due to the fact we were leaving the entire contents of the house to the gentleman who bought it I was of the opinion that we would have very little to pack – not so, nothing could be further from the truth, due to lack of storage space on the boat we had to be brutal when it came to sorting wardrobes out. Once again, Viv was having second, third, fourth and possibly fifth thoughts; she would look lovingly at some of her finer outfits, almost with a tear in her eye, as they were confined to the bin bag. When, after many rethinks and hours of soul-searching the mountain was reduced to an ant-hill, Viv, accepted this with a heavy heart and she agreed it was for the best.

With this massive emotional, and physical clear out, one item slipped my mind. I played drums, my pride and joy was a classic 70s Ludwig Vistalite five piece drum kit with extras. This amounted to seven heavy cases, a small mountain. The word hypocrisy comes to mind, I had been preaching to everybody that they should only take what they can carry... Well a good friend of mine came to my rescue, his name was Trevor, he was the guy that we met up with when we first arrived in Devon, he still lived in Exeter. He told me that he would be quite prepared to let me put my drum kit in storage unit, and that he would look after it, ad-um-infinitum.

We envisaged this project would take maybe three to three and half years, so we had some wiggle room, nothing was etched in stone. Due to the fluidity of the project, there were no hard and fast rules or schedules, but we would definitely be sailing very close to the wind .Viv and I had to find a home for the dog. During my time driving for the laundry I visited HMS Raleigh in Torpoint many times, there I struck up a friendship with a kindred spirit, Sandy. She was originally from Liverpool and now she was an instructor for the newest recruits into the

Royal Navy. Her husband, an ex-serviceman, who was disabled was at home alone when Sandy was on duty – they decided the dog would be great company for him. We brought Fluke to meet them, they bonded instantly, Viv was really happy that we had managed to find a good home for the dog. There was also one other benefit of my friendship with Sandy as my eldest son Christopher was in the Royal Navy, and he was stationed at HMS Raleigh. All new recruits do their basic training at HMS Raleigh, she was able to arrange for me to be admitted to the VIP area for his passing out parade, that made me very proud of him, and eternally grateful to Sandy.

4

Now the dog problem had been solved, that just left the cat Tibbles, she was a house cat, so she was used to being indoors and using a litter tray, and on the plus side, every ship needs a cat.

In the blink of an eye the moving date was upon us, we all made our farewells. Viv got quite emotional saying goodbye to her house. We formed up the convoy and headed south to Wadebridge, and into a world that would be radically different from anything that we had ever experienced before.

Wadebridge is a little town that sits on the River Camel – its bridge spans the river at its narrowest point, this is as far as you can sail inland. The town gets its name from the bridge. In the past, Wadebridge had a history of shipbuilding. Just along the harbour road, on the quayside, was Terry Erskine steel yachts, this was still a working boatyard. Terry designed and built steel boats. His famous boat was the Golden Hind class of steel sailboats. Next to Terry's boatyard is quayside motors, this was the garage that permitted us the use of water and electricity. Further along the quayside is Victoria House, this was the warehouse of an Artisan gift maker, his name was Paul. Oddly enough he was from Birkenhead, my home town, quite a nice little community going on here, there was also Ted, a retired farmer, whose retirement project was a converted lifeboat.

On the other side of the river there was a foundry and metalworks. It is hard to imagine that a sleepy little town like Wadebridge, somehow had managed become the hotspot for industrial espionage in the 80s, due to the fact this foundry was being used for the casting of a top-secret, much talked about winged keel, that was being fitted to the high-tech sailing yacht that would be competing in the next America's Cup – just think they also made some of my fittings.

Also currently lying alongside was the fishing vessel *Pleiades*, this was being refitted by Terry Erskine and his engineers. This vessel had a little history: the current owner, Johnny Beer, affectionately known as "mouse" had bought this boat on a Saturday afternoon in a pub, when the current owner was due to have his boat seized due to an unpaid fine. Johnny Beer, put the money up and the boat was his. He was a mining engineer, and as almost all of the mines in Cornwall had long since ceased production, he had decided on a change of career and became a fisherman.

Wadebridge had ceased to be a viable working port due to the constant silting of the riverbed. It was not navigable, one minor detail we had overlooked, the ship was high and dry and leaning against the wall. Bearing in mind we needed 10 1/2 feet to float, there would be times when, depending on the height of the tide, occasionally the ship would right herself and float for the duration of that tide, and then, due to the nature of the riverbed, there would be a very narrow window when we would have to seize the opportunity to turn the ship around, and eventually sail down the river to Padstow. This was a long way off. The original owners and builders of the ship wanted to use it primarily as a dive ship, she was fitted with 120 HP Vosper Thorneycroft diesel engine. The engine room was quite substantial, it doubled up as a workshop with plenty of workspace, and storage. She was fitted with a 400 gallon fuel tank, and a 10 gallon day tank, also a 600 gallon water tank, as well as grey water holding tank. The accommodation was laid out with five cabins, one double berth in the forecastle, with access to the sail and chain locker's, just aft, on the starboard side was a fitted galley, then on the port side opposite the galley, was single berth cabin, then up three steps, into a very spacious saloon, then down three steps and into the owner's suite, with a very nice seating area and a king-size bed. Next door was the heads and shower, the steps lifted up to reveal the engine room, just abaft of the heads along the gangway there were two more double cabins, along a gangway that also led to the navigation station, then up the companionway out onto the deck there was the cockpit, where the steering, and engine, controls were mounted. The cockpit was about 5 ft 2, and about 3 ft deep. I fitted a very nice slatted teak seat, that was hinged to allow the helmsman to stand up if he wished. We also used the cockpit, to store our LPG cylinders. Due to the volatile nature of the LPG, I also fitted a self-draining system to the cockpit. There was very little to do below decks, apart from a really good clean-up, to make it habitable.

Viv and Marlene found local jobs in care homes, Thomas started work in a fish and chip restaurant in Padstow. I was left the onboard to start the refit. The ship had 16 ton of iron window sash weights as ballast in the bilges, all of the ballast had to come out of the bilges to be cleaned, an interesting and messy job – the floorboards in the gangway had to be lifted, I was down in the bilges, passing the window weights up to Viv, she passed them to Thomas, he carried them up the companionway, then passed them to Marlene, then she would stack them on the deck, they were filthy slimy and muddy, Once the bilges had been emptied of the window weights, the next job was to clean them, this also gave us unfettered access to the prop shaft and cutlass bearings, that allowed us to carry out a very thorough examination of the shaft and it's mountings, plus we were able to grease all the bearings.

When we were satisfied that the bilges had been cleaned thoroughly, we painted the inside of the hull with a rubberised paint, I also took the opportunity to fit a new bilge pump. Also we cleaned all of the window weights, and re-stacked them on the deck.

I woke up the next day quite early. Something was not quite right, the ship was not leaning on the harbour wall, the tide was still coming in, and the ship was upright, it was quite a shock. Then I realised that, due to the uneven distribution of the weights on deck the ship had moved away from the wall. I instantly woke everybody, then got them all out onto the deck and frantically repositioned all of the window weights onto the starboard side, to make sure that when the tide receded, she went back to the original position, leaning on the wall. It is very surprising how slowly the tide ebbs, when you are watching it, then praying, that she does not lean the other way.

One of the positive points of the ship being high and dry was that we had full access to the hull below the waterline, it gave me the opportunity to check the skin fittings, and the cutlass bearing where the propeller is mounted, it also gave the opportunity to decide where to position the transducer for the echo sounder. This entailed drilling a hole in the hull, then fitting the transducer housing into the recess, then sealing it with an epoxy resin, then positioning the sender into the housing while offering a silent prayer to Poseidon, in the hope that the epoxy would keep the water out, I could not wait for the next tide, my prayers were answered, no leak!

We had shower and toilet facilities ashore at the garage, so getting the heads sorted out was not too urgent. On the day we decided to check the skin fittings. Thomas volunteered to check the outside of the hull. Because the starboard side was leaning against the wall it wasn't very bright. I rigged a light for Thomas, and put a few boards down on the mud to make it easier for him. The first skin fitting was for the galley, that was fine, he moved along now to the raw water inlet for the engine cooling, that was also fine, he then moved along to the next skin fitting, this one was for the for the head outlet. Unfortunately, the boards he was on stuck fast in the mud, he had no choice but to wallow in the mud. He got himself positioned underneath the outlet, and shouted up to me and said, 'It is blocked.' I was in the head. He told me to 'put half a bucket of water into the toilet pan.' The toilet was a Baby Blake, that is a very good brand of toilet. I put half a bucket of water into the toilet bowl, I then tried the pump. The water didn't disappear. Thomas called for a flashlight, and something he could prod up into the opening, I lowered him a flashlight, and a welding rod. He was directly under the outlet, poking the hole with the welding rod. He shouted up to me, 'More water and give it some stick on the pump.' I obliged, so I emptied the other half of the bucket into the bowl then tried the pump again, I heard this gurgling sound then an almighty swoosh, the pan emptied, I was overjoyed. I went topside onto the quay wall to see Thomas, he was up to his thighs in slimy mud, the top of his head and body were covered in whatever had been stuck in the pipe for god knows how long. He said 'I heard a gurgling sound, then rushing water, I tried to move, but I was trapped in the mud, all I was able to do, was to close my mouth and eyes. You need to give me a hand to get up on the quay, then you had better fetch me the hosepipe so I can have a swill down before I come back aboard.' I said, 'Hosepipe, you must joking, you need to be hosed down with the pressure washer, and be thoroughly disinfected before you can step back aboard.' Great stuff I said, 'We now have a working loo.'

5

Christmas came and went ,Viv, Thomas, and Marlene had been working part-time at a local restaurant, they had to work all over the holiday period, so we all had our Christmas dinner at the restaurant early in January when the restaurant was closed to the public.

The work on the ship was going very well indeed, the major problem surfaced when we realised that we had no drawings from the construction of the hull or any sail plan, or any idea how she was to be rigged, all we had were two masts.

After a long conversation with a local boat builder, his recommendation was to consult a naval architect and get some new plans drawn up. This sounded very expensive.

While I was rummaging around in some old paperwork that I had found in a box in the engine room, I came across an old invoice in the name of Michael Dodd with the home address of Trevose Head. As this was quite close, we went along to check out this address, when we eventually found the house and spoke to the lady who came to the door, she directed me to another address, informing me that Michael Dodd's mother lived there. I went to the house, the lady I spoke to there was very apprehensive, almost intimidated by me, I could see she was very uncomfortable talking to me about her son

We decided that a different approach was needed, Vivien and Marlene went back to the house a couple of weeks later to see Mrs Dodd, she invited them in for a chat, Mrs Dodd was now quite happy to talk to me. I returned to the house a couple of days later with Viv, and she was quite forthcoming, giving me the full story of the construction of the vessel, along with the grief and heartache that came with it.

Her son Michael, had taken the loss of his wife very badly, he was seeking medical advice and treatment for the very traumatic and distressing events that led to him losing his wife and then the ship. Due to the financial problems the couple experienced, there was a mention of creditors, Vivien and I were able to reassure her that the only interest we had in the vessel, and her son Michael, was purely for advice on the sail and rigging plan, Mrs Dodd said that Michael was out of the country and that she would try and contact him, we thanked her for her time, then said goodbye and headed back to Wadebridge.

A couple of weeks later, it was about 8 o'clock in the evening and we had just settled down for the night, hearing somebody outside knocking on the coach roof, I opened the hatch. There was a gentleman standing on the quayside. 'Good evening, may I come aboard please, my name is Michael Dodd.' He was with us for a couple of hours, we had a very pleasant discussion about our project, and what our plans were, he was very pleased that his dream was going to become a reality, He gave me a folder full of documents and plans, this was priceless. I now had a full set of drawings of the hull, even some pictures of when it was under construction. The hull was laid up in the boatyard belonging to Sir Robin Knox Johnston on the River Hamble. As Michael was leaving he requested that I keep his mother updated on our progress, I promised him that we would do this.

Now we had the rigging plan it looked even more daunting than it did before, he also directed me to a small foundry outside Wadebridge where he had commissioned the fabrication of the two mounting shoes for stepping the masts, and the end cap for the bowsprit, plus the bowsprit.

This was going to be a brigantine schooner, with two square sails on the foremast, three stay-sails between the masts, and a gaff rigged main, it looked very impressive. My shopping list had just grown exponentially.

I began in earnest sourcing, and finding all the materials that I was going to need to complete the rigging, steel cable for the stays, shrouds, thimbles, shackles, miles of rope, chain and countless other items too many to number, and of course, find a competent sail-maker that wouldn't expect me to sell my soul to pay for his services and all the materials that he would need.

Again an additional benefit of being alongside a small independent boatyard was that the owner, Terry, allowed me the use of his workshop as long as I paid his engineer an hourly rate for any work that he done in his own time. This worked very well, his engineer was called Chris, he was from Yorkshire, and he was very, very good, he did some sterling work for me.

The plan was to get as much work as possible done while we were still alongside in Wadebridge then we would move the ship to Charlestown harbour, I had visited Charlestown many times due to the fact that it was the home port for of a couple of the tall ships, and it was useful for getting first-hand information on rigs and rigging.

I got to know the harbourmaster Graham quite well and he was quite amiable to my request to allow me to bring the ship into the harbour to finish the work that had to be done while she was afloat. I also got to know two of the crew members off one of the tall ships that used Charlestown harbour, these two lads and worked on a number of the tall ships that had been used in various films.

Work was going very well, with the odd minor hiccup along the way, one particular occasion comes to mind, involving me, a piece of 4 x 2, and a rip saw. I came second, it was definitely my own stupid fault, I was using a portable Calor Gas heater cabinet as a workbench, this was so wrong on every level, the heater cabinet rolled, the saw crossed the back of my left hand, it was quite messy, I had to bandage my hand with a tea towel. It was early evening, and I was home alone, I came top-side, and got up onto the quay, luckily. there was a light still on in Paul's workshop. I knocked on his door, he called me in, when he saw the bloody bandage he called his GP. The GP told him that he would be at the surgery in about half an hour and that I should come round there to see him. The doctor arrived just as I got there, he called me into his consulting room, where he proceeded to clean the wound and decided it needed stitching. He said I could either go to the hospital at Truro or he would do it there and then. I agreed for him to do it, fortunately it was my left hand, after he put the first stitch in, I asked him for a tutorial, and would he mind if I continued with his guidance. He was quite amiable, so I managed to sew the back of my hand up, not much different from repairing a sail, after all sewing is sewing.

Things were moving on apace, getting to the exciting bit now, almost ready to step the masts. These masts were both in excess of 80 ft tall, what we needed was a high tide, a big crane and more importantly, someone who knew what they were doing. Mother nature kindly donated a high tide, the ship floated and she was level. The crane driver was the brother of Terry Erskine, the shipbuilder, he came fully armed with his own crane, and between him and his brother they had a wealth of experience, what a monumental couple of days.

Both of the masts were stepped and fitted, what a transformation. She went from a hull to a majestic sailing ship over one weekend. We were all overwhelmed, so much so Paul and his brother emptied their garage, and set up a large barbecue with a spit. Not sure who provided it, but a butchered lamb appeared, along with a host of other delightful treats, and countless gallons of ale. All and sundry were invited and we had a terrific time, and what a celebration.

6

During the 1984 Tall Ships' race, one of the competitors, a sailing ship called *The Marques*, came to grief not far from Bermuda, tragically 19 people were lost including a young child, whose father was the skipper.

The Marques was an old sailing ship, she was used as a sail training vessel, also, she had been re-rigged to resemble HMS *Beagle* for a television film series that she was being used in. she was also one of the oldest working sailing ships afloat, she could still carry cargo. This may have contributed to her loss. *The Marques* was struck by a line squall, this is like a tornado in reverse – the normal tornado is very narrow at sea level and goes up into the Y-shaped funnel, the vortex sucks the water up and the rotation spreads it out. With a line squall, it is exactly the opposite, the top of the vortex is narrow, all of the pressure is forced down onto the surface of the sea, creating a wall of wind. This caught *The Marques* while she was under full sail causing her to be knocked down, somehow the hatch cover was dislodged allowing tons of water to cascade into the open hold. She had sunk beneath the surface in about five minutes. Most of the crew that were lost, unfortunately were all below decks at the time and had no time to abandon ship. There were only nine survivors. Sometime later I had a conversation, with Dennis, one of the survivors, he told me of the harrowing time they spent in the water and that the most wonderful sound he has ever heard in his life was when the life-raft crashed through the surface and inflated. It had been fitted with a hydrostatic release system, that automatically launches the life-raft if it is under the water. I made a mental note to make sure that my life-raft would have a hydrostatic release system.

The captain, his wife, and family were American citizens, as were other crew members, this resulted in serious litigation.

the company that owned *The Marques* owned two other ships, one called *The Inca*, she was another old sailing ship. The second one was called *Vanessa Anne*, she was converted from a north sea fishing vessel, to a three-masted topsail schooner, she was primarily used for chartering. *The Inca* was working in the Great Lakes and there was every possibility that if she entered American territorial waters she would be impounded. *Vanessa Anne* was in St Thomas in the US Virgin Islands, and for some legal reasons, she could not leave.

During my many visits to Charlestown I became friendly with a couple of the guys that had been working on the tall ships; one guy was called Jeff, the second one was called Dick. They had both been very helpful to me while I was sourcing materials to complete the rigging.

One of the owners of the tall ships company approached Jeff and asked him could he put a crew together to fly out to St Thomas and bring the *Vanessa Anne* back to the UK. The plan was to check out the seaworthiness of the ship, make any running repairs that were needed, and then under the pretext of sailing across to Tortola to have the ship slipped, then sail off to the UK. Jeff suggested to me that maybe I should go with them, after all it would be really useful to me gain first-hand experience of rigging and sailing a tall ship. I agreed with him. I thought it was a good idea. Viv didn't think so, mainly due to the fact that they couldn't give me an exact date as to when we would be returning. After a long discussion, we decided it was an opportunity not to be missed, so I duly packed my bag. Various other crew members would be meeting up at Heathrow. As was the norm we were running late, we got to Heathrow with about half an hour to spare. We met up with the rest of the crew. There were a few bags of spares that these guys had brought with them for the ship. As I was carrying very little, one of the bags was given to me and I was asked to carry it, we had no problem with the check-in, but I did have an issue with the security desk.

During the scanning procedure, the second bag I was carrying made the machine light up like a Christmas tree, all bells and lights. The security guard asked me, 'Did you pack this bag?' I answered, 'no.' 'Do you know what is in the bag?' Same answer, 'no.' The x-ray image was showing a metallic tube with fins on one end, a coil of wire, and what appeared to be a clock-face.

I was just about to get my collar well and truly felt, when the guy who gave me the case to carry explained to the security guards that it was a ship's log. 'And just exactly what would that be?' he asked. The guy told him that 'the metal cylinder has a set of fins on one end that allows it to rotate in the water, it is connected to the wire, then lowered over the side, and trailed behind the stern. The wire is then connected to the barrel with the clock face on, this was attached to the stern rail and it enabled you to work out the speed of the ship.' The security guard was not impressed.

Once they had inspected the contents of the bag they allowed me to carry on. One of the other guys had the foresight to empty some of the items from his bag into his pockets, when we were safely aboard the aircraft he told me 'these items are like mini-fireworks that you would insert into the cylinder head of the old diesel engine, literally light the blue touch paper and the resulting explosion turned over the piston and started the engine.' 'Wow,' I said, 'if they'd of been in the bag we would have all been locked up by now.' We arrived safely on the Caribbean island of St Thomas, we all then took the bus down to the harbour at Charlotte Amalie, that is where *Vanessa Ann* was berthed. She looked weary and tired, she was affectionately known as the "Red Wreck". The engineers got down to their job and started overhauling the engine. The deck crew, including myself were allocated different parts of the ship to overhaul. My main task was to check all the standing and running rigging. The masts were very tall. My first job was to check that all of the shackles had been properly secured and to see if any of the pins needed mousing. This was done.

Fortunately I do not have a problem with heights, working aloft was not uncomfortable for me, I had a safety harness and a lifeline on, that I had secured to an anchor point on the upper section of the mainmast. With my lifeline secured I was working on one of the shrouds. But the ratline that I was standing on must of been rotten, it snapped, and I fell, unfortunately, my lifeline had fouled somehow around my neck and it nearly hung me, the drop almost ripped my head off, I'm still paying for that today.

It took four to five days maybe a week to get everything seaworthy and ready to go. I'd made a promise to keep in touch with Viv. When I got to the phone box, I gave the operator the number I wanted in the UK, she advised me to put nine dollars into the phone. I asked, 'How do I do this?' She said, 'The phone takes quarters.' I wasn't in the habit of walking round with 36 coins in my pocket – even when I had 36 coins, the problem was trying to put 36 coins in a slot one at a time, I ended up getting cut off. I decided to send her a postcard instead.

The plan was to head for Tortola under the premise of having the ship slipped, but once we had cleared St Thomas the skipper would set a course for Bermuda, which was about 1000 miles away. It was an uneventful journey, and it was really useful, I picked up lots of good tips, and help from the professional sailors.

When we were about two days away from Bermuda, Dennis the skipper called all hands on deck, the ship was hove to, and we had a small memorial service and Dennis laid a wreath on the ocean in memory the sailors that were lost when *The Marques* was sunk. He made a very touching, and poignant speech – very heartfelt especially when it was describing what it was like to be in the water, and how he will never forget sounds of the life-raft braking surface and inflating. Dennis was one of the survivors, he was the mate on *The Marques*.

We spent another week, maybe ten days so in Bermuda, regrettably, due to the time constraints that I was under, I could not spend any more time on *Vanessa Anne*. The skipper could not give me a definite date when we would likely to be back in the UK, this was unacceptable to me, so I arranged the flight home from Bermuda back to the UK. Viv was very pleased to see me, she had all sorts to tell me, I was glad to be back home, but on the positive side, I had gained a lot more knowledge and confidence to continue with his project.

Over the past six months I had made many visits to the Customs and Excise office in Plymouth, primarily it was to try get the ship registered, but we really did unearth a can of worms, due to the many complications trying to get the right paperwork, along with all the relevant certificates for the building of the hull, plus, with the circumstances of the change of ownership and the lack of a paper trail that would confirm where, when, how, and who actually built the ship.

For each problem we solved, we created an additional problem, eventually the customs officer advised me that it would be extremely unlikely that I would be able to put the ship on Lloyd's Register, this was very disappointing, and the future did not look too positive.

7

Another problem reared its head, I wanted a hand-held flare pistol, I was advised that I would have to apply for a firearms certificate to the local constabulary. I was eventually granted a firearms certificate and I was told to go to the local police station to collect it, this I did. During my conversation with the police officer, I asked him, 'Now that I hold a firearms certificate, can I buy a firearm?' He was horrified. He said to me that if I wanted a firearm I would have to choose the one I wanted, then go and pick it up on the day that we would be leaving the UK. He was still not very happy!

We had a couple of tentative dates when the tides would be right, which would allow us to sail downriver to Padstow. A couple of good friends of mine, Nick and Christine Worsley came for a visit to Wadebridge to check on our progress, and to see how we were doing. I was in a band with Nick during the time we lived in Okehampton, he was the vocalist, his young son Lee would often come to the gigs and ended up teaming up with me, helping me with the kit, packing and unpacking, he was quite a useful lad. Nick and Chris arrived for the weekend and on the Saturday at low tide we decided to walk the riverbed from Wadebridge to Padstow, mainly to familiarise myself with all the bends and curves in the river, the banks, and to see where the channel was. It took us a couple of hours. We took a change of clothes and met the girls in Padstow, we had some lunch and did the tourist thing around Padstow. When we got back to our berth, there was a very classy, sleek looking motorboat tied up at the quay. As we got closer we could see a couple of the crew members offloading a couple of boxes, I greeted the guys on the boat, and commented on the nice- looking boat they had – one of the guys answered me he said, 'Yes, she's a fine sea boat and have a good day yourself.' It was very obvious from his accent that he was from the Emerald Isle. A couple of hours later we were debating what we were going to have to eat, when we all had agreed, we decided on a takeaway. Nick and I took the order, during the course of our conversation that we were having about the boat alongside, suddenly, a thought came into my head, that something about the motor boat tied behind us was not quite right. On the various occasions that I been to the customs office I had observed various notices on the wall, one particular poster came to mind about how yachtsmen and skippers can help the customs officials spotting drug smugglers. The general consensus of opinion was that if you see something like a strange vessel somewhere that you would not normally see that type of vessel, what are they up to? This fitted the bill, a speedboat on a very quiet river, a little town, the crew offloading boxes, Nick and I put two and two together and I decided to call the customs office to report what we had seen, I went to the phone box by the bridge, spoke to the customs official and explained the situation as I saw it, he said thank you for your help, we went back aboard and had our supper with a couple of drinks, and then turned in.

About two weeks later a customs official came to the boat to discuss the registration, and in no uncertain terms, I said to him that I was 'not very happy with the response from the Customs and Excise in relation to the boat that was alongside a couple of weeks ago.' His response was 'have you any idea what happened, let me tell you. There was a crack team of SBS soldiers on your boat that night. Padstow, and the River Camel was under observation from the Royal Navy. So yes, we did take your message very seriously, primarily due to the fact that on that Sunday, the Prime Minister, Margaret Thatcher would be at the golf course on Constantine Bay, and because you mentioned an Irish connection, they thought it was better safe than sorry, so yes we did appreciate your call and thank you.

'And for the record it was all above board, the boat was being used by a local farmer who had bought some spares from Ireland.' He also said, with reference to the registration, 'Sell your boat to a non-national, then buy it back, and make sure you get a bill of sale, do that and your ship will be registered.'

When the time, and the tide had arrived we set off, Viv's sister and her husband came for a visit, and they said they would help us. Terry Erskine's brother offered his services as a pilot, he would guide us down the river to Padstow. We also had to the boys from the garage, and their children came aboard for the ride. The original plan was to sail down to Padstow, team up with Johnny Beer and his fishing boat *Pleiades*, and they would escort us out over the doom bar, then down past Land's End, then onto Fowey and finally to Charlestown.

The trip down to Padstow was uneventful, we put the pilot ashore, the two boys from the garage thought they would like to stay with us until the following day.

We cast off from Padstow, and followed *Pleiades* out of the harbour, it was a bit uncomfortable the first time in the open sea, the ship was pitching and rolling, the two youngsters were quite uncomfortable. I called Johnny Beer on the VHF told him that we would be putting about to allow the youngsters to be put ashore back in Padstow. He said 'OK.' The tide was turning, we made it back alongside with about half an hour to spare, the reluctant passengers were put ashore along with Avril and Dennis, as they had to be back in Brighton the next day. We made our farewells. and they all drove back to Wadebridge.

Then we decided we would rethink our plan. That night in October 1987, the great storm came. We were safely tucked in Padstow harbour, I shudder to think of the outcome if we had been at sea that night.

It blew a hooligan all night, fortunately we were alongside, still high and dry till the next tide, so no sleep that night.

A couple of days later, still alongside at Padstow, we had a chance encounter with a guy we met in Wadebridge, he was a sailor, his name was Jock. He had brought his boat up to the River Camel to berth her for the winter. He enquired about our trip down the river, told him we had to put the children ashore, and that we were waiting for an opportunity to continue on to Charlestown. His reply to that was, 'What are you waiting for?'

My brother Thomas and his wife Marlene had decided that maybe life on the ocean waves was not for them, they had moved on to a mobile home site, and both were still working in the fish restaurant in Padstow. We were now short handed.

Paul, the guy we met from Birkenhead also had some sailing experience, he said he would be available as crew for the journey round to Charlestown. Jock said we should go on the following day, I called Paul, his wife Anne, and drove him down to Padstow. As promised Jock turned up the next day and we made plans to go out on the next high tide. fortunately Johnny Beer and the *Pleiades* were still in Padstow harbour, and they decided to go back to Plan A, and they would escort us out. It sounded like a plan.

We cast off, and headed out of the harbour following in *Pleiades* wake. Once we were over the doom bar and heading out into the Atlantic and everything was going fine, keeping in touch with *Pleiades* on the VHF. Johnny decided to keep escorting us until the morning, just as well, the fan belt on the engine broke, and we didn't have a spare. *Pleiades*, very skilfully came alongside and Johnny's engineer came aboard, he went straight down to the engine room. He decided that we needed a new fan belt and went back aboard *Pleiades* and they sailed off. Two hours later *Pleiades* returned, with two new fan belts, at this point I wasn't aware that there was an engine spares shop in the in the Atlantic, he had acquired them from another fishing boat.

We continued on down towards Land's End, then, into the channel heading for Fowey, Jock was very familiar with the berthing facilities at Fowey – he took us alongside the floating pontoon that was in deep water so no problem drying out. Viv prepared a fabulous breakfast for one and all, the crew from *Pleiades* came aboard and, the engineer presented me with an up-to-date list of mechanical spares we would need.

We said our farewells and thanked them profusely as *Pleiades* sailed off. I had to go and check in with the harbourmaster.

Viv done some shopping. Paul and Jock went on home. Our engineer, and third crew member, Jim Harriet, an ex-bandmate of mine from up north was looking forward to joining is on this venture. He came aboard at Fowey I called Graham, the harbourmaster from Charlestown, and I told him exactly where we were berthed, he advised me that he would open the lock gates between 16:00 hours and 18:00 hours. We went back aboard and prepared to leave, it was only an hour's sailing time from the pontoon at Fowey to Charlestown harbour. We sailed out of the river Fowey, cleared the Cannis

Rock marker, rounded Gribbin Head and headed for the outer harbour. Charlestown's outer harbour has quite a tricky dogleg entrance, you have to come into the outer harbour, set a spring line, then do a sharp turn to starboard, line up the lock gate, then enter the inner harbour. As we came alongside the harbour wall, a gentleman standing on the quay offered take my bow line. He looped it over the bollard and I went aft to secure the stern line, when we were all tied up safe and secure, with the lock gate closed, Charlestown was now home for the duration of the refit.

The gentleman who took the bow line off me commented on my seamanship for safely negotiating the entrance to the harbour. I thanked him for his kind comment and his help, he looked vaguely familiar. 'You don't remember me do you?'

he said. I was absolutely amazed, it was Michael Dodd. He came aboard and he was really pleased that his dream was now a reality and he commented how good she looked we chatted for about half an hour and his final comment was 'Is she for sale?' 'No, not at the moment,' I said, now with the benefit of hindsight maybe, I should have said yes, it didn't occur to me to ask him how he knew to be standing on the quayside at the exact time that we came alongside, it was very strange .

8

Work carried on, the coach roof, and deck had been sheathed in fibreglass, very practical but not very aesthetic. I decided to lay an Iroko deck, that was a lot of hard work, but it looked fabulous. I also had good help from a carpenter I knew from Okehampton, his name was Martin Smith, he had a workshop, and he allowed me to use it to cut and plane all of the decking. Martin came to Charlestown to have a look at some of the work he wanted to do, he was not impressed with the stainless steel stern rail, he took some measurements and said leave it with me. The next time he came to Charlestown he brought with him a fabulous taffrail, complete with a beautiful balustrade, plus a full set of hand-turned spindles, along with two dozen belaying pins, it really added a touch of class to the stern of the ship.

We had been out in to St Austell Bay for a couple of shakedown cruises – the first time under the sail, it was quite exhilarating. The work carried on, the end was in sight.

We had taken her out again into St Austell Bay for some further sea trials just to get familiar with the rig and rigging, she handled very well, we were all very pleased. One day, the harbourmaster came aboard to tell me that the weather forecast was predicting a strong blow. Graham suggested that due to the possibility of the storm surge damaging the lock gates, that we should double up on the mooring lines, this we did. The road down to the harbour is quite steep, with street lamps conveniently spaced alongside the road. I released the block and tackle on the throat halyard on the mainmast, I then made a loop around the base of the lamppost and fastened the mainsheet to the loop, this would tether the top of the mast to the base of the lamppost. Due to the steep incline of the road, the mainsheet was about 20 ft above the level of the quayside, so at that height this would not impede any pedestrian's walking along the quay, it would help keeping the ship alongside, as well as leaning against the wall just in case the lock gate was damaged and the water level dropped as the tide receded, as this was a working port with ships coming in to load china clay. The water level would rise and fall with the opening and closing of the lock gate, so we had to keep a constant watch on the dock lines. Graham and I agreed that it would be prudent to keep the top mast tethered and to keep this as an additional safety measure in place. It did not impede the quayside. Occasionally I would assist the harbourmaster when he was piloting the ships into the lock. Another local lad, John, would drive the pilot boat for the harbourmaster. Graham would always advise me when the lock was going to be opened, irrespective of the time of day or night. One particular night, in the wee small hours, John must have overslept, as I was already up and about when Graham asked me to drive the pilot boat out to the coaster to let him board it. I became the relief pilot boat operator, this afforded me the opportunity to fish for mackerel on the way back, this always resulted in a fresh fish supper, one of the perks of the job I suppose.

The first mate Jim, like myself, was an ex-musician, we met another couple of musicians in the local pub the Rashleigh Arms, we had a few jam sessions and I decided that I needed my drum kit, we played a few gigs at the pub just for the fun of it, and I still enjoyed it.

The tall ship sailing company that used Charlestown as a base brought another ship into the harbour, she was an ex-pilot vessel, which provided pilots for the English Channel. She was about to be refitted as a sailing ship, we did a lot of work on that while we were at Charlestown. One of the people involved with this ship was the captain of a large clipper ship that cruised the Caribbean, he was originally from up north.

During our conversations I mentioned to him the problem I had with the registry of my ship, he was aware of the situation of a non-domiciliary foreigner owning a ship and selling it to a British subject. His wife was an American citizen, she lived in New Jersey. I sold the ship to him, he sold it to his wife, I bought it back from his wife, and got a signed, legally witnessed bill of sale, I then presented this bill of sale at the Customs House in Plymouth. Shortly after that we had a visit from a Lloyd's representative, he came to measure the ship, he issued a registration certificate. The ship was to be named *Hafan-Y-Mor*, this name came from Viv's mother, Megan, it translates to the Sea Haven, I commissioned the carpenter to carve the registration number into the main beam in the saloon. This was a momentous occasion, we were all very relieved that we were now on Lloyd's Register of shipping.

Two weeks later the full registration document was ready for me to collect from the customs office, that was a result.

We could now go ahead and secure marine insurance. Viv and I went to London for a weekend away, we took the opportunity to visit the Earl's Court Boat Show. We had a good look around, picked up a few brochures on chartering, and went to talk to a marine insurance broker. After a ten minute conversation with this broker, he asked me if we had any pictures of the ship. We didn't have any, but we gave him a good description. He asked me if this 'was the same ship that had been laid up at Robin Knox Johnson's yard on the River Hamble?' 'Yes,' I said. His reply was astonishing. 'That ship, was built by my brother Michael and his wife Anne.' He knew more about the ship than I did. The parting line was, contact me about a month before you are ready to leave the UK and we will insure you, another good result. We went back to Charlestown enveloped in a warm fuzzy glow.

We had been researching the market for chartering, we had a few good leads, and there was one that looked really promising. This was a group of whale watchers, they wanted the ship for two months in the Azores. This seemed to fit the bill, the guy that was organising the trip came down to Charlestown to check if the ship was suitable, he was very impressed, we agreed terms. He and one of his associates would join the ship a couple of days before we left for the Azores, we had about four months to finalise everything.

During our time in Charleston we struck up a few friendships with a few of the locals, and some visitors to the port, one chap in particular was a regular visitor. I invited him aboard, he was quite keen to lend a hand and get busy. He said he had done a lot of sailing in the Caribbean, he seemed quite pleasant and knowledgeable, he hinted that he would like to join us, his wife was a nurse – now that could be quite a useful addition to the crew. That would then bring our total crew numbers up to five, plus the two whale watchers, that would be seven, as we had ten berths, that would be fine during the crossing, but when we got to Horta, we would have to reduce the crew to allow the group that charted the ship to bring their paying clients aboard. We decided we could rent a small property on the island for the duration of the charter. When I passed this information to the group that were going to charter the ship, they were quite happy with this arrangement, also, they advised me that another study group were quite keen to charter the ship for another month when their charter was finished, this was more good news. The second group were marine scientists from Woods Hole Oceanographic, they were studying squid, things were certainly starting to look brighter.

We decided on another shakedown cruise, this time we were going to do a round trip to Falmouth, this was about hundred miles duration. with our crew of seven, and three more friends this would be the final test run to see how we all work together. We were ready to go, we let go the mooring lines, pushed off the wall and went slowly forward, the ship heeled over alarmingly to starboard, then she steadied herself, and drifted back, we repeated the manoeuvre, with exactly the same result. Now I was worried. Graham shouted form the road, 'you will have a better chance of making forward progress if you untie the top of your mast from the lamppost.' My reply to that was, 'Thanks, but I was just running our stability test, and yes, it passed.' He smiled, undid the mainsheet, then passed it back to me. I secured it to the throat on the boom, I thanked him for his assistance, as we gracefully sailed out of the harbour, telling him that we would be back tomorrow.

9

The sail down to Falmouth went very well, we didn't get a chance to set the square sails, we had no problems with all the fore and after sails. Falmouth is a deep water harbour with plenty of room, the plan was to anchor, have a meal, then sail off the anchorage out into the channel, set the squares and head back to Charlestown.

Tony, my soon-to-be ex-friend was on the helm, he had a compass heading to follow. Jeff, the experienced sailor was having a problem with the mainsheet, somehow it developed into a right bunch of bastards, the boom was out of the gallows, Jeff was sorting out the mainsheets. I went below to the nav station to check the charts for the anchorage and the depth.

There was a sickening lurch, the boat stopped. I climbed up the companionway to see Tony at the helm, I looked around, we were about 20 ft away from the channel marker buoy, on the wrong side of it. I yelled at Tony 'Are you bloody blind, you are on the wrong side of the channel marker buoy.' Oh, he said, 'I was following the ferryboat.' 'Ferryboat!' I screamed, 'It has a flat bottom, it would probably float in a bathtub, we need 10 1/2 feet, and we are on the bottom.' The only saving grace was, that the tide was still making, and we should be able to float off. Then came a little divine intervention. Jeff was still struggling with the mainsheet, a sharp gust of wind caught the mainsail, then pushed the boom out to about 90°, the bunch of bastards fouled in the block, the breeze filled the sail, and the ship very gracefully did a perfect pirouette, turned hard to starboard, and sailed off the sandbank much to my relief. Anybody watching this drama unfold, could not fail to be impressed with the high calibre of seamanship that was shown by the crew in handling this grounding.

Lunch was cancelled, Viv made a couple of plates of sandwiches and brewed some coffee, so it became a working lunch. We headed out into the channel, the winds were favourable, we set both the fore course and the upper course, this was the first time that we had set the square sails. She looked magnificent, we were making's about ten knots, on a very pleasant tack, this was very comfortable sailing, the voyage back to Charlestown was uneventful, apart from the grounding mishap, it was a very good shakedown cruise, and it also gave us the opportunity to set the square sails on the foremast.

Once we were back in Charlestown, the problem of what to do with the drum kit came to a head. I decided to sell the kit, so I went round to a couple of the local music stores, very disappointing results – they were offering peanuts, my pride would not let me sell them. I called my friend Nick, I asked him if Lee is keen on drumming, Nick said, 'yes, you taught him well', I asked him if Lee would be interested in having the drums. 'He couldn't possibly afford them,' replied Nick. my answer to that was, 'There will be no charge, they are free to a good home.' 'Are you being serious?' I said, 'Yes, you had better come and pick them up before I change my mind.' He arrived in Charlestown the following day, and the drum kit and I parted company.

As arranged, I called the insurance broker, Mr Dodd, to update him on our plans for leaving the UK. He advised me that he could no longer offer me insurance, on the upside, he said, 'Would you like to sell the ship?' 'No thanks,' was my reply. We were now faced with the prospect of cancelling both the charters, the downside here was I had already spent the deposit they paid, to install a radar, single side band radio, and a satellite navigation system.

I called the agent in Boston to appraise him of the situation, he told me that all of the equipment that the team needed had already been shipped to the Azores. He said it was too late to cancel and he agreed to have an independent surveyor check the ship. If it came up to their standards he would happily insure the ship for the duration of the charter. One week later their surveyor arrived, he spent the day with us, he even came out for a sail around St Austell Bay. He was happy with the ship, she was given a clean bill of health, and stated that he would recommended, that his company would insure the vessel for the duration of the charter.

The two guys from the whale watching group arrived, they brought some of their equipment with them. They stowed what they didn't want to use now and started getting their equipment ready. We had one last job to do – we had to get a compass adjuster to come aboard and make a deviation chart,

and swing the compass. This was to be completed in Carrick roads in Falmouth harbour.

On the day we were due to leave, quite a crowd turned up to see us off, Graham was given the job of piloting us out of the harbour, we had a couple of smaller boats came to escort us out as well, it was all very touching.

We sailed down to Falmouth, anchored and waited for the compass adjuster to come aboard. He swung the compass, positioned the gimbals, and left me with a new deviation, and variation chart, we were ready for the open ocean. We left Falmouth then headed out into the channel, once we had passed Coverack, we headed south-west, once we had cleared the Lizard Headland and the lee of the land, we were out into deep water.

There was a noticeable increase in the size of the swell, which increased the roll and the pitch, I checked the charts, and laid off a course for Horta in the Azores.

After about an hour it became very obvious that the latest crewmember and his wife had not been to sea before. We were sailing, the wind was fresh, with about a six ft swell, the rolling and pitching was causing this couple great distress. So much so, his wife was almost hysterical, her husband was not much better, they were both of the opinion that we were about to capsize, and that we would all be drowned. He was insisting that we call the lifeboat, or a helicopter, this went on for another hour or so, and it was clearly causing distress for Viv. She was of the opinion that he was an experienced sailor, so he must know what he's talking about, short of throwing them both over the side, I had to do something. The only thing to do was to put into Penzance, and put these two ashore, this we did, we came alongside at about midnight. The following morning I put both of them, and their belongings ashore.

Viv was visibly shaken by this experience. I took the decision to send Viv back to her parents' home in North Wales. I was able to put her on a train, with the cat, and send them both back to Ruthin. I was able to reassure and convince her that *Hafan-Y-Mor* was safe and seaworthy, and that I would contact her when I was back on terra firma in the Azores.

While we were alongside in Penzance we met a young fisherman, his name was Mike.

Mike came aboard after, a brief chat he explained that he was looking for a new job. The trip to the Azores sounded

just what he was looking for. I signed him on as our new crew member he fitted in perfectly, his young age belied his experience.

It was some 12 days later that, after an uneventful, successful, 1500 mile, voyage that we made landfall at Horta in the Azores. It was dark, I was very wary about entering a strange harbour at night. That apprehension was justified when the helmsman called to say that he could see the harbour entrance light, and that it was red. I checked the chart and confirmed that it was the harbour entrance, I told him to keep it on his port side, a couple of minutes later he said that the light was now green. I decided that we should heave to, and wait for daylight before we attempted to enter the harbour. Two hours after sunrise we were safely alongside the harbour.

After clearing customs and immigration, I was able to get to a telephone and call Viv and let her know that we had all arrived safe and sound. She was very relieved. On my first journey ashore I was very relieved to solve the mystery of the changing harbour light, the helmsman had been looking at a set of traffic lights on the dock road.

The first group were due on board the following day – there were six guests, plus the two guides, so there was no urgency to find shore-based accommodation. The first group came and went, they enjoyed their experience, it was decided that I would fly back to the UK to pick Viv up during the second group's visit. My flying date had to be brought forward due to me sustaining an injury to my elbow, I flew from Horta to Lisbon, I had to overnight in the airport departure lounge. I eventually caught a flight to the UK, I arrived in London at about 22:00 hours.

I could not have planned it any worse, some sort of transport strike, no trains or coaches, luckily, I got a lift as far as Birmingham, the guy dropped me off on one of the slip roads just off the M6. I promptly stuck my thumb up and waited. A motorist did stop for me, he asked me, 'Where do you want to go?' 'As close to the M 54 as possible please.' When I got in, I told him that I'd been travelling for the past two days from the Azores, and that I was heading for Rhyl in North Wales. His answer to that was, 'Give me the address, get your head down and I will give you a shout when we get there.' I phoned my sister-in-law Sue, and told her, 'There will be two for a late supper in a couple of hours, see you later.'

Viv had been staying with her sister and brother-in-law Bob, they lived in Kimmel Bay. We arrived at about midnight, Viv was very pleased to see me. Sue had prepared a nice meal for us both, Bob made a handsome donation to the driver's petrol fund, I thanked him profusely, and he went on his way, random acts of kindness tend to restore your faith in human kind.

10

The following day I had my elbow treated, a few days later I was fit, the, batteries well and truly recharged, and we ready to go. I had a return ticket, that plane was full. Viv had to get the next flight. Now to the seasoned jet-setters this would not cause any hardship, but Viv had never flown before. The description of being a nervous flyer would be wasted on her, she was terrified, and the fact that I was not going to be with her just magnified her fear, suffice it to say, she was not a happy bunny. My flight arrived about two hours before Viv's flight landed, so we missed the connecting flight to Horta. I found a hotel for the night and went back to the airport to wait for Viv. When she landed, she had problems due to the fact she was carrying the cat – the cat had all its paperwork up to date but the Portuguese customs officer did not speak English. Viv was put in a small office while the official tried to sort out the permits for the cat. Viv's blood pressure must have been off the scale, when it was eventually sorted and she was released, she gave me the gist of the conversation, it sounded very much like there is an import levy, some sort of fine. To me, it looked like the age-old custom of palm greasing. This was Portugal, still recovering from the Salazar regime, a very heavily policed state were the odd backhander often went unnoticed, thank heaven for the Carnation Revolution in 1974. The cat, Viv and I were all finally reunited. We checked in to our hotel, then we had a couple of large brandies, and when Viv had finally managed to relax, we had a half decent meal, then went to bed to get ready for the early start tomorrow. We took the flight from Lisbon to Horta, all went well, sort of! The pilot was quite keen to show all the passengers how interesting the runway looked from above, he banked sharply so that everybody on board could get a good view, the runway looked the same size as a postage stamp. Viv's apprehension returned with a vengeance. I'd never noticed the runway before when I took off from there, when the plane landed every passenger, including us, spontaneously gave the pilot and crew a stirring round of applause, it was with much relief when we got off that plane. Due to the fact this was classed as an internal flight, we did not need customs, so no chance for another bribe here then.

I had found a really nice apartments in the town, the owner Tino, worked in the local bank, he was the bank manager, he became very useful when transferring funds from the UK. When we were not aboard with the whale watchers, we spent a lot of time with Tino and his family, they became good friends, and our own personal tour guides for the island.

They took us to the huge crater, Caldera, which is part of the Faial Natural Park, it was spectacular, they also took us to the Western end of the island to where the huge Capelinhos Volcano is located. The last major eruption was in 1957, and the landscape was positively lunar, really odd – occasionally you would come across the top of a chimney pot sticking up from the ground, the rest of the house, and all the other buildings had been buried by lava and ash. At one point we were actually standing about 200 yards from the sea, this was new land it came up from the sea during the eruption. We also attended a couple of the local festivals, with traditional dancing and food, all out in open air. During our downtime we took full advantage of the time we had to keep in touch with family and friends in the UK. We constantly updated them, and kept them fully informed as to how we were coping with the change of lifestyle.

One of our friends from Okehampton that had helped us with some of the fine carpentry was Martin Smith, he had always expressed his desire to spend some time with us on one of the various passages. I told him that when the charter was finished we would be heading for Madeira, and, if he could find the time, he would be more than welcome to join us for that leg. He was quite keen, and said he would get back in touch within a week or two.

As the different groups changed over there would be times when the boat was empty – that gave Viv the opportunity to come aboard and do the housework, this she enjoyed, she even came out on some of the whale watching trips, which again she enjoyed, she was feeling quite at home now. We had about a week's downtime when the first charter group finished, then we were waiting for the second group of scientists, this was definitely a more professional scientific study rather than just whale watching – they were studying squid.

There were four marine biologists, and they employed a local Portuguese fisherman for catching the squid. We did not need the shore-based accommodation any longer so Viv and I, moved back on board, we also had to provide the food for them, so this was, a full board charter.

This went very well, the fisherman would go off on our tender to catch his squid, he would come alongside, then transfer the squid to the scientists. They would implant radio transmitters inside the squid, then place them back into the water, then follow the radio signal. It was a type of sonar, they could follow them for two, maybe three days, they would chart the various depths that they reached. One interesting fact we learned is that squids do not like light, during the day they dived deep, probably feeding, when it was dark they came closer to the surface. This throws doubt on the theory that when commercial boats fished for the squid, they string rows of powerful lights along the gunwales to attract the squid, also, if one of the squid that was being tracked suddenly dived deeper at speed, it was safe to assume it had been swallowed by a sperm whale, squid are the staple diet of sperm whales.

The squid we were catching were about a metre in length, these were very young. Squid have suckers on their tentacles for holding its prey, and a vicious looking, parrot-like beak. The beak is the only part of the squid that the sperm whale cannot digest. One of the scientists gave me a squid beak to hold, it had been removed from the stomach of the carcass of a sperm whale that had washed up on a beach. It was removed when they did an autopsy, it was the size of a football, the scientist told me that the squid this belonged to must have been in excess of 80 ft in length, a real monster of the deep.

Some of the squid died during the process of implanting them, the upside of that was fresh calamari. One particular squid was just about to die when it wrapped one of its tentacles around my forearm, the fisherman severed the tentacle, it was firmly attached to my wrist, I was about to remove it when, the fisherman advised me to leave it until it went limp – if I tried to force it off, it would have taken most of skin off my wrist with it, all of the suckers have tiny beaks that help them to hold on to their prey. I had to wait until my newly acquired squid bracelet had literally dropped off, then I cooked it, and ate it. The scientists were quite satisfied with the ship and the crew, they said they could use as again early next year for a new study in the Caribbean.

One of the scientists recommended that we visit St Maarten in the Caribbean; he was of the opinion that we would have no problems getting marine insurance, this was reassuring.

The harbour wall in the marina was festooned with murals depicting visiting vessels, apparently this was a local custom, and was deemed unlucky not to comply. We followed the local custom, and we were all pleasantly surprised to find that our engineer Jim possessed a hidden talent, the mural was very impressive, if it had not been done on concrete, I would have taken it with me. The ship was restocked with food, fuel, and water. When we were ready to go, I called my friend Martin to give him the dates when we would be leaving and, when we would be due in Madeira. He arrived in Horta three days later. We had also struck up a friendship with an unemployed local fisherman, he said that he needed a passage to Madeira, so he would have a better chance of finding work, as on Madeira there would be more opportunities for him. It seemed a logical reason, so we agreed he could work his passage, and as both of the islands were Portuguese there would be no immigration issues, so now we had a crew of five. The passage to Madeira is about 750 nautical miles, which should take about eight to nine days, I had previously relayed this information to Martin, he was quite happy with that. We did have a favourable weather report, so we gave the ship a final overhaul and made ready for the next passage.

11

We left Horta heading for Madeira, on the second day out the wind picked up, it was quite strong, and a six to eight ft swell, we shortened sail, lowered both of the jibs and the mainsail, then set the lower stay sail, rigged lifelines along the deck, even took the precaution of rigging a lifeline the length of the saloon.

As the day progressed, so did the wind, it was getting uncomfortable. As day turned to night, the apprehension increased. Viv had the foresight to make a stack of sandwiches and wrap them in cling-film, along with a couple of flasks of coffee, it was going to be a long night.

Martin was quite happy at the helm, he had on his foul weather gear and a safety harness, he was okay. Viv was below in the lower saloon, she was coping very well with all the rocking and rolling, the only thing that caused her a bit of distress was when, during a particularly hard heel over, the port-hole became submerged then she was imagining what it must be like to be a submariner, apart from that she was okay, it didn't appear to bother the cat either. I put my oilskins on, grabbed some sandwiches and a flask and went topside to check on Martin –he was still enjoying himself, except, for when the lightning flashed, and he looked up and could see a massive wall of water. It is always difficult to accurately guess the height of the waves, he was convinced that the waves were higher than the masts. We knew that the top of main mast is 75 ft above the deck, he said that it didn't bother him as long as he didn't see it. I gave him the coffee and sandwiches. Then I went around the deck to check the lifelines, I was just about level with the coach roof when I slipped and banged my foot on the gunwale, I lost my balance and fell, I held on to the grab rail that I had fitted on the coach roof, the ship heeled violently to starboard, I was horizontal, my legs went through the guardrail, with both of my feet almost in the water. It seemed like an eternity before she righted herself, all I could think of was, that I was really glad I fitted that grab rail to the coach roof. When she did right herself the momentum threw me in a heap against the coach roof, but at least I was still on board.

It was blowing a hooligan all night, big winds, big seas, this was the time I was really expecting Vivien to say, it is time to get me off this ship, but surprisingly, she was okay and it didn't put her off.

With daylight, the wind dropped, still big seas 15–20 ft swells. We had taken quite a battering, and also we had a lot of seawater in the bilges, we were still quite a way from Madeira. I checked the chart and the sat nav and found that we were only about half a day away from the island of Santa Maria. This was one of the smaller island in the Azores archipelago, it was about 220 miles SE of Horta. According to the chart, there was a small harbour Forte De Sao Bras. We altered course and headed for Santa Maria. The size of the harbour wall was incredible. My Portuguese friend and I took our passports and paperwork to the tin shack that passed for the harbourmaster's office, I was really grateful that I had a Portuguese-speaking crewmember, the harbourmaster spoke no English, until he found a weird discrepancy with Martin Smith's passport. The harbourmaster had a list of wanted criminals from Interpol, unfortunately Martin's name came up on this list, and to compound the problem, this wanted criminal had the same date of birth, I had to go and fetch Martin and bring him into the office, after some frenzied telephone calls and a very long two-hour wait, they were able to establish that, the Martin Smith on the Interpol wanted list was not the same Martin Smith as my crewmember. Due to having the benefit of an interpreter, we were very surprised to learn that, along with quite a few of the local fishing boats, we had just experienced the remnants of Hurricane Felix. although it was very unpleasant and uncomfortable, on a more positive note, we now realised that both the ship and the crew would be able to handle any further problems that we may encounter. We went back aboard, stayed alongside while we completed the running repairs and returned all of the seawater from our bilges back into the ocean. Viv prepared a superb meal which we all thoroughly enjoyed, then we retired for a good night's sleep. We would set off first thing in the morning to continue the voyage to Madeira.

After a couple of hours sailing a small grey bird, looking a bit like a dove, landed on the ship and perched itself on the lifeline, the lifelines were still rigged from the stern, to the mainmast, to the foremast, then on to the pulpit, we also thought it prudent to leave it in place. The bird had made itself at home, the cat was always on a harness and line, it viewed the bird as a potential meal, the bird seemed to know just exactly how long the cat's lead was, so it managed to keep just out of reach. As the bird got bolder it moved along the perch, when it got to the hatch it moved inside, still perched on the lifeline. Viv duly reduced the length of the cat's lead – they would glare at each other, then the bird started to eat and drink and it stayed with us until we arrived at Madeira.

When we came alongside we cleared customs. Jorge, our passenger and Martin both left the ship, as did the bird, it just flew off, not so much as a thank you for its board, lodgings and passage.

There was not much room in the marina, the harbourmaster directed me to a berth on the commercial quay, we made our farewells to our departing crew members, secured the ship, and gave Jim a couple of days off. He promptly went ashore, and in the time-honoured tradition of shore leave, he found the nearest pub, and got absolutely legless. This was not unusual, like myself Jim was an ex-musician, and he was quite partial to a drop of rum and coke, we ran a dry ship, so as it was his time off, so go for it Jim. Viv and I went ashore to do the tourist bit, filled in the postcards, found the post office, then we went into a little bistro and had some food, I had an omelette, Viv had a fish dish, her meal was okay. About an hour after leaving the bistro I started to feel a bit queasy and decided it was time to head back aboard, just before going aboard I was violently sick. I only just made it down to the head, and it was definitely a case of Montezuma's revenge – as soon as I got off the head, I had to do a down on my knees, and heave away, this went on for another hour, I was a basket case.

Viv was insistent that I turn in immediately, I didn't argue, it was about one o'clock in the afternoon, the next thing I remember is that Viv is shaking me, telling me that the harbourmaster was on the quay and he wanted a word with me. I wobbled topside, he was very belligerent and could not under-stand why a sail boat was berthed on the commercial quay and not in the marina, this was not the same harbourmaster who directed me to this berth yesterday – he advised me in no uncertain terms that there was a freighter coming in, and that I must vacate the berth immediately, I decided that if we left the harbour we could sail out to the anchorage, drop the anchor, and wait it out there, the only flaw with this plan, was that Jim, my other crewman was comatose in his bunk, and no amount of shaking would rouse him. I went below to the engine room, checked the day tank and that the raw water inlet was open, started the engine and went back topside, Viv was on deck, the harbourmaster threw both the bow and stern lines aboard. Viv coiled them up and stowed the fenders, there was plenty of room in the outer harbour, with the engine idling we were just about making headway. Viv came into the cockpit and took the helm, there was nothing else that I could do, so I told Viv to keep her eyes open, while I went below to the nav-station, I checked the charts. I came back on deck and gave Viv the heading that I wanted her to steer.

I then went forward, set the inner jib, and one of the staysails, then went back to the cockpit to check that Viv was happy, then I went back down to the nav-station, to check the charts, and laid off a course for Tenerife, it was about 270 miles away.

I came back up on deck to make sure that all was well, and that Viv was okay, she was absolutely fine, and she was insistent that I go back to my bunk and get my head down, I followed her advice and went back to my bunk. It was about 1530, I was sort of dreaming, and I could hear Viv screaming, 'Mike, Mike, Mike, get up here now.' I was still half asleep and bleary eyed, I stumbled along the passageway, and made my way up the companionway. With my head and shoulders poking up through the hatch, I was half in and half out, Viv was still shouting, and I mean really shouting, all she kept repeating was 'look, look, look.' I swivelled my head from side to side, expecting to see a supertanker bearing down on us, but I couldn't see anything. She yelled at me, 'Get up on deck and look.' I did, and WOW, I could now see why she was so excited, we were surrounded by hundreds of dolphins of all sizes, they were calling to each other, leaping, doing somersaults, Viv told me to take over the helm, as she went below to get her camera, she took dozens of pictures from every angle, at one stage she was even hanging off the bowsprit trying to touch the ones that were surfing our bow wave. When she came back to the cockpit she asked me, 'How do you feel?' I replied, 'Much better thank you,' was my reply. I asked Viv, 'What is the time?' She answered, 'It's about eight-thirty or nine o'clock.' I was shocked. I said to her, 'Have I been asleep for nearly five hours?' She laughed, 'It's closer to 15 hours, it's 9.30 in the morning.' I was amazed, Jimmy was conspicuous by his absence. 'Where is he, Is he still in his bunk?' Viv said, 'Yes I think so, I have not seen him all night.' I went below to wake him and put the kettle on.

I continued on to the to the nav-station, I was amazed to see that we were still on course and that we had made excellent progress through the night. Viv had made the grade as a helmsman. I made us all hearty breakfast and Viv turned in to try and catch up on her beauty sleep. The rest of the day was uneventful, perfect sailing weather, it was also a good learning curve, it was hard work, but we found that a crew of three can run the ship. I would not like to do it too often, but at least we didn't need anybody else, this was a good feeling.

12

The next couple of days went very well, the weather was fine, calm seas and good visibility, Tenerife was easy to spot, thanks to Pico del Teide at just over 12,000 feet tall, difficult to miss. We sailed up to Santa Cruz, it looked like a very busy marina, it was quite crowded, as this was the set off point for the Atlantic Rally for Cruisers. We sailed further up the north-east coast until we came to the fishing harbour, Darsena Pesquera, this looked ideal. We checked in with the customs, and harbourmaster, and we were allocated a berth alongside a disused freighter. This freighter had a couple of open wooden boats tied up alongside, we had to reposition them to allow us to come alongside, we put one of the wooden boats against our starboard side, the other one, we just moved it along so it lay astern of us. We had a stand-pipe, and an electrical hook up point, all the comforts of home.

We settled in to life in Tenerife with great ease, we had about seven to eight weeks before we set off for the Caribbean, time to get in some good relax-ation, and to catch up with any other maintenance tasks we needed to do in order to keep everything shipshape. As per usual we struck up a relationship with a couple of the locals, Carlo and Roberto, they turned out very useful, and a great help for driving us around the island sightseeing and shopping, also finding any engineering, and rigging spares we needed.

This harbour in its heyday would have been very busy with fishing boats, now it was not so busy, up on the next berth to us, there were two, Korean registered factory ships, they looked tired, I don't know how long they had been alongside.

One crew member told me that the ship had been impounded, due to not paying harbour fees, he also said that the crew had not been paid for ages. It is impossible not to feel sympathy for these sailors, being stranded in a foreign port with no money, and no chance of contacting their families. Or getting back to their home port.

We had arranged for an additional five crew members to join us, they would be paying for their passage to the West Indies.

We planned for a 40 day passage, with another three or four days, as a contingency, we planned the menus for one day, once we had worked out exactly what we needed, we multiplied it by a factor of 45, on paper that looked like an awful lot of stores, but fortunately we had ample storage facilities. Viv took on the mantle of chief cook and bottle washer. The stores were her responsibility, she decided to revamp the storage system. Viv's reputation for housekeeping is legendary, I joke, almost OCD, she went through the store system like a tornado sorting out what she wanted, what she would use on the voyage, and finally what she did not want. I was somewhat concerned at the size of the pile of the items that she had discarded. When I had the audacity to question her, the reply was that 'they have all passed their sell by date.' We filled up three large boxes, then struggled to get them up on deck, she then deposited a bottle of rum in each box, now I was confused. I was always of the impression that age improves alcohol, she then went to the next berth and spoke to the captain of the Korean ship and presented him with the three boxes with our compliments. The captain and the crew were very grateful, the next day we were invited aboard for a real nice meal, Viv and I were the guests of honour at the captain's table. The captain and the crew showed us their appreciation in their own way – over the next few days various items were deposited on our deck, two coils of rope, boxes of shackles, engine spares, engine oil, filters, and as much diesel fuel as we could carry. This confirmed my belief that, you reap what you sow. There were quite a few sailing vessels in the harbour that were getting ready for the Atlantic crossing, there were lots of dogs in and around the harbour, unfortunately most of these had been abandoned by their owners before they set off on the long voyage. As was the norm, Viv would put food out for the strays, one day she said to me, 'Aren't the Korean sailors kind, they are feeding the dogs.' I didn't have the heart to tell her that tomorrow the dogs would be feeding the sailors.

Everything was going well, all of the ongoing maintenance had been done, the one thing we had learned was that the sails needed protecting from chaffing against the stays and shrouds, we started a new cottage industry, making baggy-wrinkle, we ended up giving lessons to some of the other boaters, somehow it's very therapeutic sitting in the sun turning bits of old rope into fenders and sail protectors. We wanted to get to know our new crew members before we set sail, we could not afford to take the chance of a repeat performance of the debacle when we left Falmouth. We made sure that they were all present and correct at least one week before we set sail. There was Manfred, a retired ship's captain, he had retired early, he wanted to spend some time in the sun. There was another Manfred, he was in his early 20s and had done plenty of sailing. They were both German, the next one was a Dutchman whose name that I could never pronounce, needless to say he was christened Dutch, he was in his 30s with a couple of Atlantic crossings on his log which I checked, it looked to be all in order. We had a friend from the UK, Maggie Clark, she was from just outside Okehampton, she had become a good friend while we were living in Okehampton, I used to do some work on their farm, on her bucket list she wanted to sail across the Atlantic, she went on a couple of shore-based courses, and a week's practical sailing aboard a yacht to familiarise herself with life afloat. On the sailing course she was on she met a guy who was of the same opinion that she was about crossing the Atlantic – she then asked, if it would be all right if he came along, she assured me he was okay, and that he didn't have two heads, and he was alright in the confined quarters of a boat. We had decided that, if for any reason we did not all get along, whoever was at fault would disembark at the earliest convenience – bearing in mind it was over 800 miles to the Cape Verde Islands, then we would just have to put up with them until then. My son Christopher was still serving in the Royal Navy, he had been injured, and after surgery, he was recuperating in the naval hospital in Plymouth. The M.O. had just finished his rounds and he was talking to Christopher. He told him that he needed 'plenty of exercise and some bracing sea air to speed his recovery.' Christopher's reply was, 'My father and stepmother are in Tenerife at the moment, just getting ready to sail across the Atlantic Ocean to the Caribbean on their sailing ship.' He asked the M.O. for permission to join us. The M.O. replied, 'Leave it with me.' He came back later and said to Christopher, 'If you can guarantee me that you will be back by January 2, yes you can go and join them.' We had crewmember number nine. This worked out very well, he replaced Viv on the watch rota, that, in turn, freed Viv up to concentrate on being a galley slave. We devised a watch system that was quite easily managed, we had four watches, two crew to each watch, four hours on, twelve hours off. The watch that was stood down during mealtimes became honorary galley slaves that were able to assist Viv. I had been very specific with the prospective crew members, as to the amount, and quantity of their baggage and personal belongings that they would be bringing with them, bearing in mind additional storage space was at a premium. All other crew members complied with this request, with the exception of one, Manfred – during our correspondence and subsequent phone conversations he had requested permission for him to bring his windsurfer. I decided that would be OK, as we could store this in the tender, alongside the bags of fresh fruit and vegetables that we carrying. The tender was mounted on its storage bracket on the coach roof. The Canary Islands, are the final staging point for the Atlantic Rally for cruisers. This is a gathering of sailors, and sailboats, of many different shapes and sizes, there were 200–220 sailboats getting ready for crossing the Atlantic, and heading for the Caribbean, we picked the sailing date, then spent the last couple of days getting everything ready, and making sure we were as prepared as we can be, we set off, made our farewells and said goodbye to Tenerife, next stop, who knows.

13

The weather was fine, the ship sailed very well and we soon turned into a very competent crew, the watch system worked very well with everyone getting enough sleep, there was also plenty of spare hands available if any situation arose where extra hands were needed. there was always plenty to do for the watches that was stood down, so not much chance for boredom to set in. The galley service was excellent, Viv done a sterling job, amazing one and all with her culinary expertise.

Freshwater was not a problem, the ship's water tank was used for the galley, I had purchased ten 25-gallon containers, each one had been labelled with the crew member's name on it then filled with freshwater, then they were all lashed to the stern rail, the freshwater was to be use for whatever reason needed. When we encountered a squall, it was all hands on deck to bathe, whether you needed to or not, we also rigged a modesty screen on the fore-deck to allow the ladies a little bit of privacy, not that there was much chance of doing anything privately in the claustrophobic confines of a sailing ship.

We had even been able to devise an elaborate water chute that allowed us to collect rainwater, it was also ideal for topping up the crews' personal containers, and when they were all full, we would top up the main tank.

The course we were taking meant that we would be quite close to the Cape Verde Islands, they are a couple of small archipelagos about 400 miles west of Senegal, we had a full tank of fuel, and plenty of water so it wasn't critical that we stop, it just seemed like a good idea at the time. We headed for, Mindelo, the main port on San Vicente, as we came alongside, we were greeted by about two dozen locals all vying for the privilege of securing our dock lines to the bollards, difficult choice. Once the choice was made we became aware that, with our two new shore crew, we had also purchased the services of two watchmen. I went to the harbourmaster's office to clear customs and immigration. It was Friday, late afternoon, the customs officer wanted all of the passports, he also told me that he would be sending another officer to check the ship, and our inventory, this other officer duly arrived at our berth and commenced his measuring ritual to ascertain exactly what they would charge us for being alongside, the figure was eye watering, not sure what system he was using but, I think he might have confused us with the *QE2*, and I am eternally grateful that we didn't have to make use of their bunkering facility. Shortly after another officer appeared, he was the official photographer, he advised me that he had to take a photograph of every crewmember, when I questioned this, he said this was standard practice, and it enabled then to compare the photograph with the passport pictures. I suppose that in a Third World country, that must make sense, what didn't make sense was the fact that he insisted on taking a picture of the ship's cat, these pictures also had to be paid for, the cost of being alongside was rising quicker than the tide. Now for the inventory, he checked everything, engineering spares, ropes, life-jackets, and when it came to the galley stores, I was made to feel like I was running a food smuggling racket, needless to say we ended up having to make up a couple of gift hampers, well it was December.

I told him that we would be leaving in the morning, he said that's not possible, the office will not be open until Monday – great, a fabulous fun-filled weekend in Paradise. The two watchman informed me that they needed, warm, waterproof jackets to keep them comfortable through the night, and also, they would require a hot meal. I advised them that it would not be necessary for them to spend the night on deck as we would not be going ashore, that didn't make any difference. I thought it prudent to lose two waterproofs, than to run the risk of losing anything that was a screwed down – during the hours of darkness there was always one of my crew members on deck.

I gave half of the crew the day off on Saturday, and the other half, the day off on Sunday. First thing Monday morning I presented myself at the customs office to buy my passports back, the parting words from the customs officer was, I hope you enjoyed your visit and please come back anytime. I was very relieved when my two new best friends were able cast off the dock lines and we headed out.

I am convinced that if the Almighty ever decided to give the world an enema, this is where would shove the tube.

We soon got back into the rhythm of life at sea, everything back to normal, the winds were fair, we had all the sails set, including the squares on the foremast, the trade-winds were constant, so no trimming of the sails, or running round pulling ropes, the helmsman was made redundant, we were able to lash the wheel, and occasionally just to relieve the boredom occasionally steer by hand.

Considering that there were around 230 boats making this passage we did not see a single sail. We did monitor the VHF, and occasionally the SSB but we had no contacts. At about 16:00 hours, on 15th December I saw a distress flare, it was on my watch, and a couple of the other crew members also saw the flare. We took a fix with the handheld, entered it in the log, altered course, then called all hands on deck, sent two crewmen aloft, one on the foremast and one on the main, and started to search. We put out a call on the VHF we did not get any reply, we searched until the daylight faded, we did not find anything, we went back to our original heading. The mood on board had changed, it was quite subdued. The following day we reset the squares and continued to make good headway.

The fresh water and the stores were lasting very well and everybody appeared to be enjoying themselves, none more so than Manfred Jr and Christopher. They had rigged up a bosun's chair and fixed it the yard arm on the main course, they took it in turns to swing out, one would go as far forward as possible, sit in the chair, and kick themselves off, the other one would be waiting midships and try to catch him. It looked like fun, but they soon tired of it, a bit boring they said. The next scheme was a little more challenging, this involved the same bosun's chair, this time it was fixed to the end cap of the bowsprit, they measured the fall so that the bosun's chair skimmed the bow wave. This time they tied themselves onto the bosun's chair, under full sail we could make around eight knots and depending on the swell they would occasionally be submerged. To be tied to a small piece of wood and dragged through the waves at eight knots is not for the faint hearted, being keel-hauled comes to mind. While he was in the water, Christopher must have come into contact with a jellyfish, because he had a terrific angry looking rash on his thigh. This caused him to limp for a day or two. One other problem we experienced, albeit a pleasant one, was the flying fish. During the night, when they were being chased by bigger fish they would leap out of the water and some of them would land on the deck, at night you couldn't see them but you could certainly hear them, they would end up in all the smallest inaccessible places. The downside was that if we didn't see them, they rotted very quickly and the smell was awful when we found them.

Herman, said they make good eating if you catch them fresh, the problem was, that we were competing with the cat – we never got any fish, but the cat was very well fed. On the 24th of December I was on the midnight watch with Viv keeping me company, when a really vicious squall blew up. Because of the dark I didn't see it coming, for the next ten or fifteen minutes it was blowing a hooligan. I was seriously considering calling for some help to shorten sail when the wind abated, and it was back to normal, with much relief. My watch ended at 0400 hours. Christmas Day, Viv and I went below to get a few hours shut-eye, then it was party time. Viv spent about four hours in the galley, she produced a feast, there were prawn cocktails, soup, and a pâté, there was no roast turkey, but we had a terrific steak and ale pie. It was decorated with a large pastry turkey, it tasted as good as it looked, we had all the traditional vegetables, pigs in blankets, stuffing balls, and the gravy was to die for. She also managed to produce an absolutely outstanding Christmas pudding, made with dates, raisins, and mixed dried fruits, and to top the feast of she produced a huge platter of mince pies, we celebrated Christmas, and toasted Viv, with a glass of wine.

14

We made our first landfall on Boxing Day in Barbados. It was late afternoon, it was quite surreal that after 29 days at sea the first landfall we make is exactly the same as Christopher Columbus made in 1492. It must have looked the same to him as it did to me. We came alongside at the customs berth in Bridgetown, went in with all the necessary paperwork and we cleared customs without any problems, we sailed round to the Anchorage in Carlisle Bay. We had arrived in the Caribbean with a full tank of fuel and plenty of water, as well as ample foodstuffs in the ships stores, that was a successful crossing. The next couple of days was spent catching up with all the maintenance for the running and standing rigging and checking that everything was okay. Viv, also got in some good relaxing time, and she was looking forward to going ashore and having a decent meal that she had no part in preparing. We found a nice restaurant in Bridgetown. Viv said she really liked the look of the flying fish on the menu, when her dish arrived it looked amazing, she was very pleased. Unfortunately, she put quite a lot of Bajan hot sauce on her fish, it burnt her mouth, but she was determined to finish the dish, she was drinking milk for the next few days. As we were at anchor, the tender was put to good use going back and forth to the jetty as the various crew members made their arrangements for going back home, or to continue their travels in the Caribbean. We also had a reunion with our shipmate from Padstow, Jock. He was most upset, he told us he had spent two weeks touring the Canary Islands looking for us, he was of the opinion that he would be joining us for the crossing. He had flown to the islands from the UK with the intention of joining us, he ended up buying 32 ft steel sloop called *Cygun* from a sailor who at the last moment decided he was not going to make the crossing, Jock sailed single-handed but he was in constant contact with a young British couple, who were on a 24 ft fibreglass sloop. He said they left Lanzarote with the bulk of the fleet about a week before we left Tenerife, he also confirmed my theory about the Cape Verde Islands. Apparently the day before, he had been in a bar room brawl with a couple of the locals, this did not surprise me. He said it was his first day ashore, and had one or two large rums. Jock was a useful lad, an ex-merchant mariner, he was no stranger to the more seedy watering holes that sailors in foreign ports always seem to gravitate towards. This time, unfortunately, one of his protagonists used a knife, the resulting wounds to his abdomen needed hospital treatment, when he was told how much the hospital wanted from him he just left, went back to his boat, took out a sail repair kit had another large run, and proceeded to stitch himself up. That was Jock.

On or about 29 December, Viv and I took Christopher to the Grantley Adams airport for his flight back to the UK. He said he had thoroughly enjoyed the trip, and he felt fit, and fully recuperated, and ready to go back to his job with the Royal Navy. Maggie Clark, and her friend had left the day before.

Maggie got quite friendly with our other crew member Jim, he decided to go back to the UK with them, that left just, Viv and I on board after everybody else had left. Jock had taken us to one of his favourite watering holes, where lots of the sailing fraternity use the establishment as a sort of clearing house, must be the West Indian version of the job-centre-cum-travel-agent, we met up with a South American sailor called Molino. He was working as crew on a sailboat in Bridgetown, he invited us a board for a meal and a chat, he seemed a likeable sort of chap and he put us in touch with a couple of guys that needed a lift to Saint Lucia, and another youngster from Sweden, his name was Magnus, he was a diver. Molino, Magnus and the other two Frenchmen came aboard. The next leg was to Saint Lucia, which is about 125 miles south-west of Barbados. Just before we left we had a word with Jock, he said as soon as he was fit he would be leaving himself and heading for St Maarten, and that maybe we should look each other up there. That sounded like a good idea, we told him to look after himself, and that we would see him in maybe a month or so. We set off for Saint Lucia, for another idyllic day's sailing in the Caribbean. It was now official, we were now living the dream. We arrived at Rodney Bay, anchored in the lee of Pigeon Island, went ashore in the tender, cleared customs and immigration and put Molino and the two Frenchmen ashore. Magnus stayed aboard with Viv, when I returned, we decided that we should all go ashore and have a look around. We took a cab to Castries, had a good wander round the town, and then on to Soufriere, and to see the Pitons, we then found a nice restaurant and went for a meal. Viv was a little more careful with the hot sauce this time. We stayed in Saint Lucia for about three days, out and about playing the tourist. The next port of call on the itinerary would be Martinique, it was only about 60 miles from Rodney Bay, so if we left early enough we would make it in daylight. The plan was to leave at about 0400. Everything went according to plan we left Saint Lucia heading due north to Martinique. We headed into the anchorage at Fort-de-France Bay just after 1800 hours with enough daylight left to find a suitable place to drop the anchor for the night. We had a light supper and turned in. We went ashore in the tender, cleared customs and immigration, then had a look around the town. Martinique was very French, hardly surprising this was France, wandering round an open-air market we bumped into Molino, he said, that he was 'looking for a passage to St Maarten, and could he join us?' 'Why not,' I said, 'we will be here for another couple of days, then we will set off.' He was okay with that, put his gear in the tender, and came back aboard with us. Later on in the afternoon we caught our very first fish, it was a big red snapper, we all had a delightful fish supper. The anchorage at Fort-de-France Bay was quite crowded, there was a veritable forest of mizzen and mainmasts. Due to our size I would always make a point of finding a suitable place to anchor well away from other vessels, this usually meant a longer jolly boat ride to go ashore, but it left me plenty of sea room. We were all woken up quite early by the frantic shouts of a very charming, but distressed French lady who had been left the on board a large catamaran with two very small children. Her husband and the rest of the crew had gone ashore for provisions. The catamaran was dragging its anchor, and it was heading straight for us, and it looked like some sort of collision was inevitable, fortunately, the shrouds of the mizzen on the catamaran made contact with our yard arms, this prevented any hull contact, but then we started to drag. Molino managed to get aboard the catamaran, while Magnus went up the main mast to the yards, between them they managed to separate the rigging, Molino was able to start the engine on the catamaran, he was able to retrieve the anchor, then they was able to move to another position, then reset their anchor. The French lady was very grateful. Later. when the crew from the catamaran came back the captain came over and presented us with a case of wine, and a very sincere thank you.

Later. The following day we suffered the same fate, the anchor must have been disturbed, so now we are dragging, the wind had freshened, it was offshore, so no cause for concern really, I just didn't like the experience of the anchor dragging, then, as if by magic, the anchor found decent holding ground and we stopped. Not being a believer of divine intervention, I thought that this was a bad omen, so I decided to make ready for sea, and make full use of the offshore breeze, we slipped the anchor, and headed for St Maarten.

15

The passage was not uneventful, we experienced some sort of collision just off the coast of Dominica, not sure if we hit something, or something hit us, it was dark and then we felt a very loud thump on the starboard side just amidships. A full check, did not reveal anything amiss, unless you consider losing the tender as nothing amiss.

The following day all went well – the weather was fine it was good sailing, the wind was picking up and it was getting stronger. During daylight we shortened sail, took in the outer jib, and put one reef on the main, we were still making a good headway even with the shortened sail. We went below for supper, Viv was getting ready to turn in when I said I was going topside to check that the boys were okay. Molino was on the helm, he had told me he had plenty of experience sailing, and that he was planning some sort of business venture when he arrived at St Maarten. The other crew member, Magnus, he was a young skanda-hooligan who had escaped the endless darkness, snow, ice, and permafrost of his hometown, Umea in the north of Sweden. He was also a professional diver and he was looking forward to securing employment in one of the many marinas.

I had completed the evening rounds, then went below to join Viv. About an hour later Molino called me up onto the deck, he had picked up a red light just off the starboard bow. I followed the line of his outstretched arm and confirmed it was a red light, I went below to the navigation station, looked at the sat-nav, copied the coordinates on to the chart, and confirmed the island was Nevis, and the red light was the harbour, at Charlestown. We were about three miles offshore, I went back on deck relayed that information to Molino and told to keep on that heading, I went below back to my cabin. Shortly after I heard and felt a sickening crunch, all forward motion had stopped, the ship was heeling over to starboard. I ran back along the gangway and up the companionway and out onto the deck, the sight that greeted me caused me great confusion as to why ship was no longer underway, and why was she was heeling severely to the starboard side. I got to the helm, Molino said, 'I think we have run aground.' I shouted to him, 'How could this be when we are in deep water?' He panicked, he went to the stern rail on the port side and hung on to it like his life depended upon it. I jumped down into the cockpit, the relief that I felt when the engine started was palpable, I put the controls to ahead, opened the throttle, then turned the wheel hard to port. The relief that I felt soon evaporated, there was no response to the hard over wheel, I moved the wheel and it spun to freely, the ship was being pounded from the waves crashing on the port side. I climbed back down the companionway to the navigation station, grabbed a flash light then I had to remove the panel behind the companionway to gain access to the tiller flat. The flashlight illuminated the interior of the tiller flat, I was horrified to see that the steering cables had somehow come adrift from the rudder quadrant, this obviously happened with the first grounding. The rudder must have struck hard and subsequently jolted the whole steering quadrant forcing the cables to come away from their housing. It was impossible to try and thread the steering cables back into the channels on the quadrant due to the effect that as the waves hit the rudder, the quadrant was flogging wildly and there was every possibility of losing a couple of fingers or even a hand. The final solution was to take the emergency tiller topside, open the access panel in the cockpit, and steer the ship manually – words cannot convey the sheer desperation that I felt when it became obvious that the emergency tiller handle, did not fit on to the boss of the rudder post. This was a new tiller handle that had been cast in the foundry when we had a bell cast, the tiller handle had some rough edges on the receptacle, and it would not fit, my engineer Jim, told me that he would attend to it, obviously another one of the little jobs he didn't get round to. Every so often a bigger wave would smash into the hull, the gross weight of the ship was in excess of 60 tons, yet the raw power of the wave would lift the hull and push it further on to the reef and we were heeling over at an alarming angle. It became apparent that the ship was lost and there was nothing else we could do to save her, the main priority now was Viv and the crew. I told Molino and Magnus get into their life-jackets, and be prepared to abandon ship, I went below to Viv, who at this time took it all in her stride, she was very calm and collected, I told her to 'get the go ashore bag and a life-jacket.'

I went aft to make distress call, put out a Mayday on Channel 16. Somebody did answer. I advised them that I was in distress and about to launch the life-raft with four crew members, the message came back, please clear this channel, I'm a taxi driver. The next wave was a big one, the resulting push, heeled us further over, the rack holding the batteries in place must of given way, all power went, instantly turning everything into inky blackness. I made my way back to the main saloon. Viv had a life-jacket on, her major concern was the cat. Viv had a hold of it, but it was not a happy cat, clawing, spitting and biting, I didn't relish the idea of an angry cat being inside the life-raft. I took the cat from Viv and started to put it into the go ashore bag, this was a large two handled holdall type bag, ideal as a grab bag. This bag contained everything that was important to us, ship's papers, passports and cash, the cat did not want to go in the bag. It was pitch black, with lots of water crashing in from the open hatch, at this time it felt like the cat had grown another set of legs, it was like trying to post an octopus through a letter box, it was clawing its way out of the bag, as I was trying to force it in. Lots of other things came out with the cat. I eventually managed to stuff the cat in the bag and close the zip. I went topside, the crew had launched the life-raft and they were in it, the life-raft was secured to one of the stanchions. I threw the bag into the life-raft, then I went back for Viv. Due to the angle of the deck, it was difficult to stand up right, the starboard guardrail was underwater with waves crashing all over the deck. I got to the hatchway, and as I leaned in to help Viv, to my horror the steps up to the deck had carried away. It would take a superhuman effort to get Viv out, yet still she was very calm. I managed to squat down above the hatchway, reach in, take both her hands in mine, and physically hoist her out onto the deck. I hauled on the painter to pull the life-raft in close, she was able to board the life-raft. Just before releasing the painter, I looked around trying to get an idea of exactly where we were, I could see lights off in the distance, also more alarmingly, the life-raft was amidst sinister looking rocks. I decided at that moment, that I would not board the life-raft, and that I would stay in the water and somehow try to guide the life-raft safely through the rocks. Both the life-raft, and myself were repeatedly bounced off the rocks, which resulted in both the life-raft and me getting repeatedly punctured by the coral.

I managed somehow, to cling onto the life-raft despite being buffeted by the wind and the waves. It is very difficult to try and put a time frame on the situation that I was now in, I was convinced I had been in the water for an eternity. Then, an overwhelming feeling of relief that washed over me like a warm fuzzy glow – in that instant, when my feet touched the sand, and a couple of minutes later, the bottom of the life-raft crunched onto the sand.

16

Viv and the two boys climbed out of the raft, and pulled it further up on to the sand, it was at this point when I thought that Vivien had really lost it, she was physically trembling, and really upset when she saw me. It didn't sink in with me at first, but I must have looked as if I had just received a hundred lashes. Although, all the cuts, scratches, and scrapes were superficial, the loss of blood, mixed with seawater, made it look a lot worse than it was. This part of the island was uninhabited, the lights I could see in the distance were maybe a couple of miles inland, I had to go for help.

I set off into the bush, and it might as well have been deepest, darkest Africa. It was pitch black, no path to follow, I kept stumbling, tripping, and falling over occasionally. I was still in shock, my senses had not yet come to grips with the enormity of the situation that I was now in.

It was impossible to imagine what kind of wild animals that I had disturbed, as they were now crashing through the undergrowth. My imagination was running wild. I eventually came across a dwelling, it was all in darkness. I repeatedly knocked on the door, without getting any reply, I carried on up the hill, things looked a little more hopeful as the next dwelling had a light burning, I knocked on the door, an elderly lady answered, she was a little bit bewildered, almost afraid of someone knocking on her door in the middle of the night. She refused to come to the door. I told her that we had an accident and we needed some help, she said she would phone her daughter. Her daughter told not to open the door, and that she would call the police. About half an hour later a police vehicle arrived with two police officers. When I explained the situation to them they told me to get into the car and they would take me to the police station. I pleaded with them to take me back to the beach so that I may pick up Vivien they were not too sure, they eventually agreed and we set off on the road that would take us down onto the beach. When we got there they saw the life-raft and my crew, there was not enough room for everybody, so the two boys said they were quite happy to stay with the life-raft till the daylight. Viv and I went off with the police officers back to the station and we were able to sample Nevisian police hospitality, this left a lot to be desired – granted, we were two white people who had come in very close to the shore at night, we did fit the bill for drug smugglers, or people traffickers and we were treated accordingly, so much so, that when Viv wanted to use the bathroom an armed female officer escorted to the cubicle and made sure she didn't close the door. The duty officers were not sure whether we were criminals or just unlucky, they said a senior officer would be arriving at about 7 am so we just had to wait. It is surprising what you will read when you're bored – the noticeboard was filled with applications for liquor licenses. What was chilling, was that most of the applications were for the town of Charlestown, I asked the police officer exactly where we were, his reply was, 'you are in the police station at Charlestown', I thought how ironic, Charlestown was our home in Cornwall, that was the start of our voyage, and now the voyage ended in Charlestown.

Now in daylight, we had another major shock when we discovered that during the harrowing time we had getting Viv and the cat off the ship, most of the contents of the go ashore bag, including all our cash, were no longer in the bag.

The dream that was cherished, and nurtured for all those years, was now well and truly shattered. The police sergeant arrived at the station just before 7 am, after a brief conversation with him, he was under no illusion that we were still very traumatised, and our current surroundings were not conducive to our well-being. Fortunately this officer had spent many years in the UK police service, the first thing he did was to drive us back down to the beach to pick up the crew members. During the drive back to the beach we explained to him how, and where, we came ashore, he was quite surprised, and then he told me the chilling news, that 'not many miles up the coast is the municipal dump, and this attracts sharks into the shallows at night, judging by the wounds you received in the water you are very lucky to be here talking to me now.' We were mortified. We got down to where Magnus and Molino were still waiting, when we picked them up, he drove all four of us to a local hotel and at his own expense, and put us into two rooms where we could wash, change, and have some breakfast. When I explained to him about the red light we saw last night, I told him that I was convinced that we were in deep water, at least a couple miles offshore, and when I checked the chart, it confirmed the red light at Charlestown harbour. He then told me, that due to Hurricane Hugo, there was lots of damage to the islands infrastructure including, roads, power lines, and hundreds of domestic dwellings.

The radio mast was also destroyed, and that an emergency radio mast had been constructed out of scaffold tubing, and because of aviation regulations, a red light was fitted on the top of this mast. This was a contributory factor to me misreading the chart, and wrongly assuming that this light was at Charlestown harbour.

As the owner of a British Registered ship, that is on Lloyd's Shipping Register, I am liable for an indirect taxation called light dues, which I paid in the UK. This money goes towards the upkeep and maintenance of navigational aids. The fact that there were no maritime navigation lights working at the time was definitely a major contributory factor, leading to the loss of the ship. The police sergeant introduced me to the immigration official, who also doubled up as the official receiver of wrecks. He said to me that 'the government's position would be that, while they would be very sympathetic to me over our loss, they definitely would not accept any liability.' He also said that they would also grant me a work permit that would allow me to find a job. I was very grateful to him and thanked him profusely.

For all the wrong reasons we became instant celebrities, the owners of one the plantation inns, I think it was called the Hermitage, came to the B&B that we were staying in, and insisted that we come to their hotel as their guests, the kindness of their gesture did not go unnoticed, we were very touched. There is a small community of expat Americans that come to Nevis for their holidays, one lady in particular, her name was Judy Blackington, each year she came to Nevis for a four-week holiday. She would rent the priest's house at St Theresa Church on Main Road. Judy is a single lady, and this was a big house for one person – she was adamant that we should come and move in with her until we found suitable accommodation for ourselves. She also organised a bring-and-buy sale, and an afternoon tea in her garden, along with a charity auction, with all the proceeds going to our rescue fund.

17

We were able to contact Viv's family, needless to say they were horrified at the thought of Viv and I washing up on a beach in the Caribbean, with only the cat and the clothes that we stood in, just like a modern day Robinson Crusoe. At least we still had the cat.

Bob, my late brother-in-law, he was married to Viv's sister Susan, they very generously offered to pay for our return passage back to the UK. We had just learned that Susan and Bob's house, along with most of the other residents of Kinmel Bay, Towyn, Pensarn and Abergele had suffered the most catastrophic flooding that has been seen in North Wales for many years, part of the seawall carried away, coupled with spring tides, a low barometric pressure, and high winds, flooded thousands of houses. They were dealing with their own massive problems.

The idea of being homeless, jobless and penniless, in the damp, cold mountains of North Wales, compared with the warm, sunny, white sandy beaches of the Caribbean – it was a no-brainier really, at least we didn't need, overcoats, boots, or umbrellas.

We made the decision to stay for a while to see how things were going to turn out. Magnus, somehow had acquired a full set of diving equipment, he went back to the wreck site, and successfully retrieved some of Viv's personal belongings including some of her jewellery. When a vessel comes to grief, all sorts of odds and ends wash up on the beach, this usually ends up as rich pickings for beachcombers – the local Nevisian's that lived close to the beach. And at this point it's worth remembering that most, if not all of them lost many personal items, and many of them had also lost their homes due to the damage sustained from Hurricane Hugo. If anything that resembled our property washed up on the beach, it was all collected, and deposited at St

Theresa's Church, actions like this tend to restore your faith in human nature. Nevis is a tiny island in the eastern Caribbean, its bigger sister is called St Kitts, these islands are separated by a two mile wide channel, called the narrows. The name Nevis, is derived from the Spanish, Nuestra Senora de las Nieves, which means, our Lady of the Snows. The island is dominated by a dormant volcano, known as Nevis Peak. Legend has it that Christopher Columbus gave the island its name because when he first saw it, the peak of the volcano was shrouded in white cloud, and from a distance it looked like snow. The mainstay of the island, is the tourist industry, there was a large resort under construction for the Four Season's Group. The main contractor was a company out of Montreal, called Jaltas, they brought their own skilled workforce, and they provided a lot of opportunities for the local Nevisian's. At Judy Blackington's garden party I was introduced to one of the managers, JP. since I had just been granted a work permit, he offered me a job in his workshop. I was overjoyed. Another friend of Judy's who was at the tea party was a gentleman named Bob. He knew the owner of a block of holiday apartments and he paid the rent for one month for an apartment for us. We adjusted to the Nevisian lifestyle with the practised ease of seasoned travellers. I was given a start date, and off I went to work. I worked in the machine shop making all the decorative gingerbread, and balustrade panels for the balconies. It was a very physical job and I would work 55 hours per week. I think this job prevented me from turning into a basket case. It was hard work but I enjoyed it. We were also able to find a real nice apartment just outside of Charlestown. I was earning enough now buy an airline ticket for Viv to go back to the UK and visit her family. All the arrangements were made, the flights were booked, and I took Viv to the Vance W. Amory International Airport in the village of Newcastle. This did sound impressive, but it didn't look as good as it sounded – it was a small airport, with equally small aeroplanes, affectionately known as Island Hoppers. This did nothing to improve Viv's perception of aeroplanes and flying. Had there been an alternative method of leaving the island, irrespective of what it cost, I'm sure Vivien would have opted for that. She was planning to be away one month, that would give her time to visit her sister in West Sussex, then up to North Wales to see her parents, her brother, her other sisters, and their families. She had also arranged to meet up with my son Christopher. Vivien, does not like flying, she likes it even less when she is alone. Vivien had a few health issues in the past, couple this with being an nervous flyer, and just for good measure, add all the pressures and the stress of the past few months and eventually, it all caught up with her and she was quite unwell. The flight crew were brilliant with her, upgraded her to first-class, and she was first off the plane, albeit wheelchair-bound. Viv's sister, Avril, and her husband Dennis, were at the gate to meet her – she was quite happy to be back on terra firma. They all drove up to North Wales and Viv said that she felt like a homecoming Prom Queen, she was able to spend some quality time with her family and her younger sister Nerys, threw a party for her. Christopher managed to spend the weekend in North Wales and he told Viv that he would try his best to come out and Nevis for a visit as soon as he could arrange it. Viv spent her last couple of days back in West Sussex with her sister Avril. This worked out very well as she was flying from Gatwick. On the day of her flight, she done her last bit of shopping, she was quite cryptic, and would not disclose what she bought, the only clue she would give me was, it for you. Christopher's girlfriend, Sarah worked for British Airways, she had pulled some strings for Viv, she had been upgraded to business class, so far so good, she had checked her baggage in, still good, then her whole world collapsed – when she had to produce her passport at the immigration desk, the immigration officer told her that her passport was invalid and she could not travel with it. We had a joint passport with both our names and pictures on it, the immigration officer advised Vivien that she could not use the passport when travelling alone, and he could not understand how she had been able to travel from Nevis to St Kitts, then on to the UK without any customs official checking her passport. Vivien explained that all due process and been followed and the passport stamped without any questions being asked, the bottom line was that Vivien could not travel with that passport, she had to get one of her own, her ticket was cancelled, and she had to apply for a new passport. The passport office were very helpful, and due to the circumstances, they would use their express service to process the application. The express service was still going to take one week, there was absolutely nothing she could do. She had to surrender the current passport in order to get a new one, this was done and her flight was booked for the following week, the downside to this was when she got her luggage back she had to dump the surprise that she had bought for me, ten pound of Walls finest pork sausages. Vivien returned to Gatwick with her brand-new shiny passport, so far so good, no problems with immigration this time, she still had an upgrade, and to ease the pressures of the flight, she was even taken onto the flight deck to meet the pilots, all went well, the flight duly landed at St Kitts airport that's when things started to go downhill at an alarming rate. When Vivien surrendered the old passport, it also contained the necessary work permit, and residency permit stamps, you cannot land in a Caribbean country, without the means of leaving that country, unless you have a valid permit to be there, you cannot come in with a one-way ticket. Viv had no way of getting hold of me to let me know what was happening, the immigration officers at St Kitts were quite adamant that Viv would not be allowed to stay, the only problem was, she had no means of going back to the UK. She then remembered the dealings we had with the immigration officer on Nevis, somehow she had even managed to remember his name, she pleaded with the officer in St Kitts to call the officer in Nevis, this he did, and between both of them, they finally agreed that Vivien would be allowed into St Kitts, then be able to fly into Nevis. The officer from Nevis, via a government employee, whom I had become friends with, managed to get a message to me to tell me what time Vivien would be landing at the Nevis airport. This friend gave me a lift to the airport, we arrived with about 20 minutes to spare, so we had a couple of beers in the international departure lounge, well just outside, actually it was more like a beer shack than a departure lounge, on the plus side, as there were no windows, and without even trying, you could hear every word that was being said in the building, including the radio conversation between the pilot and the landing controller: (pilot) 'just cleared St Kitts, over'; (controller) 'OK I see you now, over'; (pilot) 'will be with you in about four minutes, over'; (controller) 'that is fine, see you when you touch down, over'; the plane lines up the runway... (pilot yelling) 'the grass is too long, I cannot see the landing light, over.' I watched, as the plane's wheels touched the runway, then lifted off again, turned around, and flew back to St Kitts. I had a word with the controller and he assured me that the grass would be cut for tomorrow, and that the two passengers will be booked into a hotel on St Kitts for the night. He also gave me the telephone number of the hotel that they would be staying in, in St Kitts. When I eventually got through on the phone to Viv, she was furious. 'Can anything else go wrong?' she said. I told her 'There is an alternative, if you get a cab to Basseterre, you can catch the ferry to Charlestown.' But due to the mix-up with immigration she decided to stick with the original plan, and fly in the next day, what was really upsetting her was my gift, Walls finest pork sausages. When she left Avril's house the sausages were frozen solid, due to the BA cabin crew being so helpful they put the sausages in their freezer.

They were now in a hotel freezer with a guarantee they would be handed to her as she left the hotel for the airport, I was very impressed, I didn't realise she was so resourceful, and all of this because I missed a proper fried sausage. We said good night and I promised that I would pick her up tomorrow. She was very relieved when she stepped off the little aeroplane, I gave a huge hug, and she couldn't wait to get back home and put my sausages in the freezer, it was quite an eventful trip – as well as feeling unwell on the original flight to the UK, combined with all of the immigration problems with the passport at Gatwick, then even more immigration problems upon her return to St Kitts, and finally, the fiasco at the airport when she had to fly back to St Kitts, all in all, quite a traumatic experience. She was very glad to be back in the comfort of our home, even the cat was pleased to see her.

18

We became firm friends with a couple of ex pat Brits, that had made Nevis their home, Mike was a retired marine engineer, whose previous skill's set, made him an indispensable asset for the local government owned power plant. Mike was originally from Cornwall, as well as being a ship's engineer, he owned, flew, and maintained his own vintage biplane back in the UK. On one of his trips into the port of Liverpool, he met, fell in love with, and married Christine, one of the barmaids who worked in his favourite pub, they were a great couple, we would barbecue every weekend, one weekend in our garden, the next weekend in their garden. Mike worked with a lot of the locals, most of them came to his barbecues, this in turn helped us fit into the community. Once we had settled into our, apartment, we decided that we would like to do a big barbecue as a thank you to everybody that had been so helpful to us, we did a rough headcount, and decided they would be about 45 guests, that seem like a lot of chicken legs, sausages, and jacket spuds. Mike suggested that we build a big barbecue with a spit, and roast a couple of goats, or a pig. This appeared to be a good idea, we picked a couple of tentative dates, then he took me into the bush to meet the local cattleman. This guy told me I could have one of his pigs. He brought one over to me, and said, 'This one will do, and I will get it ready for you on the day you want it.' I paid the man, and went away quite content. We contacted Christopher told him what the plan was, he would confirm the date that he and Sarah, his girl-friend, would be coming for the holiday, he also asked me if there was anything I needed. I told him I could always use some power tools, he told me he would put a package together. We had about three weeks to arrange things that seemed okay. As we started to make plans a couple of the Trinidadian guys I was working with offered to build the barbecue for me, they said it would be ready a week before we needed it. We were woken up very early on Sunday morning by someone banging on the front door, bleary eyed. I answered the door, there was a young boy standing there with a piece of rope in his hand, he didn't say a word, just gave me the rope and he left. There was a sharp tug on the rope, I was still half asleep, the rope was trailing around the side of the house. I slipped on my shoes, and went outside. I pulled on the rope, and to my surprise, a pig trotted into view. Bloody hell I thought, your almost three weeks early. I went back indoors and told Viv that we had a visitor, and that she needed to go out to the garden now. She was besotted, it was love at first sight – in our house I come a close second to the cat, now I had just gone further down the pecking order. We couldn't keep the pig in the garden, we only rented the apartment, fortunately, there was plenty of spare land around the house that the pig could graze on. There was also a large tamarind tree that would provide some shade, and stop it from getting sunburned. I secured the pig to the tree with a chain, this gave it plenty of freedom to move around. I was surprised how intelligent the pig was, if the chain was fouled around the tree trunk, and I placed the water bucket just out of reach, the pig was able to walk around the tree trunk, and unravel the chain to reach the water bucket. Vivien would see that it got fed at least three times a day. During my lunch break, one of my colleagues was just about to throw an apple into the bush, he said 'it was going bad.' I asked him for it, he said to me, 'Why do you want bad fruit?' As I put it in my bag, I told him, that, 'It is for the pig.' The next day, I had more fruit and bread than I could carry, we had a very well fed pig. Needless to say, as the day we had chosen to visit the butcher arrived, Vivien made it very clear she would take a very dim view of anybody who ate barbecued pork, and that included both Christopher and myself. We had asked everybody who had said they would come to the barbecue to bring a case of beer. Most people brought two, we had over 80 cases of beer, countless bottles of rum, gallons of wine and tons of food. It was a banquet fit for kings, we had a sort of rota for turning the spit. The pig had been well wrapped in tinfoil, occasionally the cry would go up, 'Pigs on fire.' that prompted an instant response, and resulted in two or three people emptying bottles of beer onto the carcass to douse the flames. It worked, barbecued pork, with the beer marinade. I took the risk of falling foul of Vivien, and I had a couple of slices of pork, it was delightful. We think Christopher's serving may have been slightly underdone, as he was unwell for a wee while, he thought he might have been jet-lagged but, being a tough old salt, he soldiered on, and kept on drinking rum and coke under duress. The barbecue was a storming success, everybody enjoyed themselves, and we were really grateful to be given the opportunity to express our gratitude to everyone who had helped us. Christopher and Sarah enjoyed the rest of their holiday with us, they were quite sad when it came time to leave. Christopher had also brought me some new power tools, I was very grateful for this. When they left, it was back to normal. I had managed to take a couple a days off in order to spend some time with Chris, but now it was back to the grind, working ten hours a day, and half day on Saturday, not that I am complaining about it, it did pay the bills. One guy I got friendly with, Bill, was working as an engineer for the plant and machinery on the site. He and his wife Linda were from America – I was not very sure of their legal status on Nevis, it would have been unlikely that they would have had work permits. Bill and Linda also ran one of the bar restaurants in Charlestown, this was called the Octagon, not a bad place to go for a drink after work. They seem like a nice couple. Viv ended up working with Linda at the bar, and she helped out in the restaurant. Viv turned up for work one day, the bar was all shuttered up and closed, which was a bit unusual, as they both lived on the property. The following day we found out that they had both been arrested and taken to St Kitts. They were charged with a drugs-related offence, they were both released on bail. I've had a few conversations with Bill and Linda, and I had no idea that they were drug users – he told me about the court appearance, and that they had been released on bail, and that they were due to reappear in about six weeks' time. Bill was of the opinion that Linda would plead not guilty, and with his knowledge of the legal system, he would plead guilty, make some sort of plea bargain, and he was convinced he would receive a small fine and a slap on the wrist. On their day in court, Linda did plead not guilty and her case was dismissed, she was free to go. I'm not sure of exactly how much Bill knew about the Nevisian legal system, because he denied that Linda had anything to do with the drugs, he accepted that it was him, and he apologised. He was sentenced to 20 years with hard labour, and from what he told me it was exactly that, out on a chain gang working on the roads. The prison was like something out of a nightmare, almost Dickensian, with bread and water as the mainstay of the diet. Linda, had managed to raise some money to pay a surety to have Bill released pending his appeal, both of them had to surrender their passports. It came as no great surprise to me that somehow they had managed to get some help from a fellow American sailor, who arranged a passage for both of them to the US Virgin Islands. We never saw, or heard from them again. All they took with them was what they could carry, they had to leave everything else behind. I suppose that having to lose everything they owned, as opposed to the alternative of spending the next 20 years in jail, was the lesser of the two evils.

19

Nevis was the little sister of a two island group, she was twinned with St Kitts. When St Kitts achieved independence, they separated from the much smaller island of Nevis. Nevis is still a British dependency, with its own claims to fame, with one or two, famous names from history amongst its famous sons. Alexander Hamilton is one, and in 1887 Horatio Nelson married Francis Nisbet from the Montpelier Plantation. The Nelson Museum is a must see for anyone with any nautical interest. We had decided that our future lay in Nevis, so we decided to look for a more substantial home to rent. The apartment we had was suitable at the time, now we decided it was time to move on. We found a really nice house, two bedrooms, kitchen diner, and a nice living room, a big garden with two huge mango trees, and a carport. it was close to Bath village, it was in need of renovation. I arranged a good deal with the owner for the rental on the proviso that I fixed the house up. I had some good help from my Canadian workmates, it didn't take long to bring the house up to a standard we were happy with. Viv settled in to our life, she was quite happy now that I was earning enough wages to be able to pay for the price of a plane ticket back to the UK if and when it was needed. One Sunday afternoon I answered to someone knocking on the door. I saw a gentleman standing there hand-in-hand with two young girls, he wished me good day and he told me these girls were his daughters who he come to visit, he was from St Maarten. He asked me 'if I would mind, if his two daughters went into my garden to collect some mangoes from the trees?' I said, 'Be my guest.' He said he would be back in an hour so with his car and a couple of bags. When they returned the girls collected an enormous amount of mangoes. He was very surprised when I refused an offer of payment, he gave me a business card and told me to look him up the next time I was on St Maarten. We did miss some of the basic things, difficult to put your finger on it now but the choice of things for sale in the shops left a lot to be desired. This also did not go unnoticed to a lot of my newfound Canadian friends. It was easy enough to take a ferry to St Kitts, but the was not that much more choice there. One of the guys suggested that we should charter a small aeroplane, then we could all fly to St Maarten for some real serious duty-free shopping Viv thought that that was a good idea. It worked out quite reasonable, for a full day shopping on St Maarten. We landed at the Princess Juliana airport on the Dutch side, caught a minibus into Phillipsburg. Vivien thought she had died and gone to heaven, after the frugal stores of Charlestown, this was paradise, she spent about four hours wandering around in a retail heaven. Just when she thought it couldn't get any better, we were taken over to Marigot, to the French side of the island, classy restaurants, chic boutiques full of designer merchandise, all with the duty-free label. It was definitely a shopper's paradise, and the contents of the supermarkets made as all wish that we chartered a bigger plane. Things were going well, Viv found a new part-time job in another small restaurant, and she was guaranteed a full-time job when the hotel was completed, things were looking up. My friend Mike suggested that if we were planning to stay on Nevis, why don't we build our own house? We had never really given that idea much thought, but now it made sense, there was always plenty of building plots available with some of them being quite reasonably priced. You had to find a suitable plot, then submit an application for a building licence, and a residency permit. We found a nice plot for a price that we could afford then we submitted all the applications for the licences. After about a month I received a letter from the government department advising me that I was not successful with my licence application. I met with the official to discuss this and he advised me to submit a new application for a different plot. This confused me. I asked him 'Why would an application for a new plot be viewed any differently from the original?' He told me that the new plot belonged to him, and it would be viewed more favourably. The only flaw with this plan was that he wanted four times the price of the original plot. This was way out of our reach – unfortunately most of the holiday homes are all owned by wealthy Americans who can afford to pay inflated prices for plots of building land, so that dream was shelved. As the construction of the resort was almost complete, Viv was employed by Four Seasons as a team leader, in the housekeeping department. Vivien was interviewed for her position by the executive housekeeper, Rosemary Matheson. Rosemary was a highly skilled executive who had worked at various Four Seasons hotels including their flagship hotel in Canada. Her parents lived at St Kitts and her father had a lot to do with the renovations of the Brimstone Hill fort. Viv got on very well with Rosemary. I also did some work for her at her home. She had two very large dogs. I remember building two equally large kennels for them. Rosemary described the kennels as almost Gothic – don't know what she meant. I was still employed with the main subcontractor, along with about a dozen or so members of the original construction crew. We were responsible for the snagging lists, of which there were many. This hotel was aiming for a five-star rating, so the standards were set exceptionally high. This resort was designed with their sights set firmly on the top end of the tourist market. The site of the resort is on a coconut plantation, with a fabulous golf course with the lush greens sweeping down to the palm-covered, white sandy shore line at Pinney's beach. The golf course was designed by Robert Trent Jones II. One of the minor details that was overlooked was the land crab. This crafty little crustacean lives in a hole in the ground, it has one large claw that is designed for the digging of perfectly round holes in the ground, that look strangely similar to the hole that the golfers try to knock their balls into. Overnight the 18-hole golf course, was miraculously transformed into a 40-hole golf course. This was a constant source of annoyance to the green-keeping staff. Another piece of local wildlife that was ignored was the donkey. Wild donkeys roam the sloping hills of the plantation doing what donkeys do, also, when they charge around they can do as much damage to a green as what a tractor would do. The management solution was to organise a donkey cull, this idea did not go down too well with the locals, or the paying guests, baby donkeys are really cute. The final solution was for a Western-style round-up, the donkeys that were caught where shipped to another island. Finally another problem that arose – 'coconuts'. When the coconut is in the tree in its husk, it is huge, when they fall, they cause more than a minor headache if you have the misfortune to be underneath one. They had to put a plan in place to remove the coconuts, and some of the palm fronds before they fell. This usually involved the use of a cherry picker, this was not very practical. Two local boys offered to sort the problem out physically by climbing up the tree with a machete, lopping off the fronds and the husks, then the greenkeepers could carry it away. The head keeper agreed to pay them five dollars per tree, that is EC dollars, the greenkeeper was very pleased with this price, he asked for a demonstration, and the Nevisian lad willingly obliged. He had a machete attached to his belt, and a small piece of rope with a loop at each end. He put his hand in one loop, passed the rope around the tree, the second loop on his other wrist, and he shimmied up this tree in about 25 seconds. After half a dozen swipes of his machete, I think he was back on the ground before the last coconut fell. Conservatively, he could do about 200 trees a day, he became very wealthy Nevisian. As the construction of the resort neared completion most of the crew returned to Quebec, their home town, all of the equipment and machinery that was used in the construction was dismantled and stored in their shipping containers. The parent company was in the final stages of negotiations for a new contract on the Isle of St Marten, most of the containers were shipped to a storage facility just outside Phillipsburg in St Marten.

20

I was offered a job at the Four Seasons Resort, as Project Coordinator, in the engineering department. There was no doubt that the company were about to utilise all of the skills that I had acquired during the construction of the resort. All of the employees with the construction company were from Quebec, they were all given a very attractive pay package, they all had full expat status, and they would be exempt from local income tax, all of their accommodation, and meals were included in this package. This was a very similar package that was offered to all of the management staff at Four Seasons, all in all, it was a very good deal for them. All of the locals that were employed on the site were paid local wages, plus a bonus, again this was good pay. My situation was slightly different, because I had been granted a work permit and residency papers I was classed as local, so I was paid accordingly, and subject to local income taxes. I was earning a living wage, but my expenditure included rent and services, this made a big hole in my income – we were comfortable but it was increasingly difficult to live comfortably on a small island that is geared for wealthy tourists. The fact that both Vivien and myself were in full-time employment did help us keep our heads above water.

My immediate boss, Brad, was very sympathetic to my situation. I was offered a promotion to the position of Laundry and Valet Manager, a generous pay rise came with this position, plus a 10 day all-expenses-paid trip to the Four Seasons Hotel in Chicago. Primarily, the aim of this trip was for me to get better acquainted with the management style of a five-star laundry facility. I landed at O'Hare International, it was about two weeks before Christmas, and the weather made me realise why I wanted to stay in the Caribbean – it was freezing with snow and I didn't have a decent topcoat. I took the bus to the hotel, it was amazing, I was checked into the staff quarters, just time to get a quick shower, and to present myself for dinner the staff restaurant, that was an experience I thoroughly enjoyed. My mentor, Mike, had been to

Nevis as part of the transitional opening team. He showed me around his domain; it was a very smooth and slick operation, he even organised a visit for me to one of the engineering companies that manufactured some of the machinery that was used in the laundry in Nevis. That was a real success. I spent some quality time with a couple of their engineers and I was treated to lunch in their executive dining room after the afternoon session. I had amassed quite a collection of manuals and operating instructions for laundry equipment.

When it was time to leave, the MD asked me, 'How did you get here from the hotel.' 'I came by bus,' I answered. 'That's not going to happen, fix our visitor up with the driver please,' he said to one of his associates. I was introduced to Mary, she looked like everybody's favourite grandmother, a petite, sweet, little old lady. My opinion was confirmed during our conversation as we walked to the car pool – she proceeded to open the rear door to usher me in. 'I'd much rather sit upfront with you if that's okay.' 'Absolutely fine by me,' she said, 'are you staying at the Four Seasons on North Michigan Avenue?' 'Yes that's the one,' I answered. She told me to 'buckle up' as we pulled out into the traffic. I didn't actually see the transformation, I felt, and heard it, she must have flicked a switch, I am sure she sprouted horns and began breathing fire, as well as turning into a foul-mouthed, raving lunatic, with the odd obscene gesture thrown in for good measure. This was road rage in all its glory long before it became fashionable. I'm not sure how she acquired her driving skills, it would not be an exaggeration when I say how relieved I was when we pulled up outside the hotel. She must have thrown the switch again, because she turned to me, kissed me gently on the cheek, wished me happy holidays, and said 'Thank you for making my day, I really appreciated the chance of meeting an English gentleman.' I was speechless.

The general manager and his executives were having a presentation as their hotel had just been presented with the prestigious five diamond, five-star, award. I think at this time there were only five other hotels in the world came up to the standard. I was invited to address this illustrious gathering. I was still a bit of a celebrity due to my status as a shipwrecked sailor who washed up ashore on a Caribbean island – a modern day Robinson Crusoe, that's how I saw myself. There must of been something that was lost in the translation, for during my introduction speech, the name Gilligan kept cropping up.

I was invited to a party, it was quite a gathering of these young high-flying executive types. I was in a group of about half a dozen or so. We were drinking and chatting and one of the guys said to me, 'Do you fancy a one-hit?' In my naivete, I said 'No thanks I will give it a miss, I have got some CSR here.' One of the other guys started a conversation with me, 'What is CSR?' he asked. I started to explain to him that CSR is a white rum that is distilled in St Kitts, and that I'd brought a couple of bottles for some of the guys that were part of the opening team for the hotel in Nevis. During this conversation, just out of my line of sight the guy that offered me a one-hit had taken something out of his pocket that resembled a silver cigarette case. I was in and out of the conversation, yet I was still drawn to this guy with the cigarette case. He now had in his hand what I thought was a cigarette holder. I thought this looked a bit classy, a silver cigarette case and holder, you don't often see that in this day and age, very 1920s or 30s. He appeared to be screwing the cigarette holder into the top of the cigarette case. He now had my undivided attention. The cigarette case went back in his pocket, and he took out a Zippo lighter. He flipped the lighter open, put the cigarette holder into his mouth, ignited the lighter, then inhaled deeply. I was horrified, the guy I was talking to was rather surprised at my reaction. He said to me, 'Don't you approve of a bit of recreational use?'

Up until this point I was always of the opinion that only deadbeats and down and outs used drugs, this was the first time that I had actually seen somebody use hard drugs. I have been around bands and musicians all of my adult life, and it is, with my hand on my heart that I can state, I have never seen hard drugs being used before. I have never been a smoker, apart from a trial puff on a Woodbine behind the bike sheds at St Hugh's when I was about 13. I did not like it then, and it made me feel quite sick. Most of the musicians I would hang about with back in the day were all smokers, and they would roll their own, whether or not they would use the occasional joint of wacky baccy was beyond me, all tobacco smoke smelled the same to me. Looking back to my time in the Swinging Sixties I have to be totally honest and admit to messing about with some of the mind-altering chemicals that were readily available – once you had tried this concoction it changed your whole world, it was like living your life in a kaleidoscope, the colours became sharper almost glowing, and your hearing senses were so acute you had surround sound long before it was invented. The downside was a bit more traumatic, it resulted in bringing about major personality changes, and it did definitely induce hallu-cinations, this was very unsettling, so I made a sincere promise to myself that I would never ever drink Newcastle Brown Ale again.

My time in Chicago was coming to an end and I must say I really enjoyed the experience. Vivien had taken this opportunity to present me with her wish list, after all it was Christmas, so I didn't skimp when it came to buying her cosmetics and perfumes from Bloomingdales. I arrived back in Nevis, suitably weighed down with gifts. Viv was glad to have me back, we had a lot of gossip to catch up with. We had a couple of days off together, over the Christmas holiday. Vivien was a bit unwell, her symptoms necessitated a jour-ney to the local A&E department of the Alexandra Hospital on Government Road. She was admitted as an in-patient, and diagnosed with acute dehydra-tion. She was prescribed an IV drip to rehydrate her, the nurse brought the stand with a bag of IV solution, she fitted a cannula to the back of Viv's hand, inserted the drip and then she left. The back of Viv's hand started to swell due to the fact that the cannula had been inserted incorrectly. I removed it and called for somebody else to do it properly. Viv is not a good patient, her blood pressure was off the chart she was experiencing a fluctuating heartbeat and palpitations, it took me a couple of hours to calm her down. She was kept in overnight for observations, if she was okay I could take her home in the morning. I came back the next day and I was surprised to see that she was sharing the ward with a couple of goats – that seemed to be the norm. She made a speedy recovery at home. We both went back to work a couple of days after the Christmas holiday. This was a very busy time for the hotel as it was full to capacity. We settled into the work pattern with, both of us usually working the same shifts so our days off work were together. Finally, the last members of the original construction crew were finished, they packed up their gear and left for home, with one exception, Jean Paul Beauregard. This gentleman became so enamoured with the Nevisian lifestyle, he stayed. He had started a relationship with a local lady, Lynditta, she had a baby boy with him, she already had quite a number of children, with none of them sharing the same father. This did not seem to bother JP, he told me he was madly in love, and that he wanted to spend the rest of his days with his new extended family. As a skilled carpenter, it did not take him long to transform Lynditta's shack into one of the most desirable residences on Craddock Road. About six or seven months later, I was contacted by one of the bosses from the construction company. He told me that there was a good possibility of him landing the contract for the construction of the new resort on St Maarten, and would I like to work for him? This would involve me leaving my job with Four Seasons, and moving to St Maarten. The initial plan was for me to relocate to St Maarten and source ten or maybe twelve suitable houses, that would be available for rental to the initial group of key workers. I was told to include myself into this group. As I would be moving to St Maarten for this project, I would be entitled to the full, expat package of pay and conditions. This sounded like a lottery win, this new project was bigger than the Four Seasons scheme, and with it a guaranteed income for the next 3 1/2 years, this would really set us up financially, and would in some way, would help to put us back to where we were before that memorable night in January when we lost the ship.

21

Vivien and I had many long conversations about the pros and cons of what this new venture would mean to us in relative terms. Just when we thought we had settled into the new Nevisian lifestyle, it looked like it was all about to change again, there were many variables that had to come into the equation. We were both about to resign from our positions with Four Seasons, these were full-time jobs that were reasonably well paid, with a secure future. We lived in a nice house, albeit a rented one, and had a new network of really good friends. We also had full legal status to live and work on a Caribbean island, we would have to give all this up. The enormity of the situation that we were faced with caused us both many sleepless nights, we had to weigh up all the possible pitfalls of leaving Nevis, then compare them with the possible benefits of relocating to St Maarten. We faced the prospect of being illegal immigrants, with no work or residency permits. As British passport holders we did enjoy the benefit of free movement of labour within European Community – the Dutch half of St Maarten is independent whereas the French side of the island is a province of France, so in theory should be no problems living and working on the French side. I think this was the contributory factor that led to us making the decision to relocate. We started to put things in place and make plans for the upcoming move, once again we find ourselves in the position of getting rid of personal belongings that we are collected over the past couple of years. Once again it was time to be brutal. I made a large packing crate, one that we could easily handle between ourselves and the mantra was simple, if it didn't fit in the crate it wasn't coming with us. It took a couple of weeks to have a sort out and fill the crate, then we decided that a yard sale take care of any items that we did not want, including our treasured, Mini Moke. We gave our notice to the hotel, then we had about a month to finalise all the details of the move. We packed the crate, took the dimensions, and guessed the weight, then organised it to be shipped from Charlestown to Phillipsburg, about a week before we were due to leave.

We held a leaving party at Mike and Chris's house – one of Mike's friends was visiting them, he had a sail boat that was anchored just off Charlestown Pier, during our conversation he told me that in a week or so he would be heading for St Maarten, and that he was quite happy to carry me, and most of our baggage with him. This fitted our needs perfectly, due to the amount of excess baggage that we would have had great difficulty in fitting into one of the small aeroplanes. It was agreed then that Viv would fly with the cat to St Maarten, as it was only a half hour flight. Viv wouldn't be on the plane long enough for her to get nervous, and at least she had the cat to talk to. We were given a shipping date for the crate and the instructions for collecting from the warehouse in Phillipsburg. We had another couple of days before our final shift at the hotel, and we had a day set for our yard sale. Our final shift came and went, and it was with much sadness that we bade farewell to all our work colleagues. Once again we were overwhelmed with the gener-osity of the proceeds from our yard sale, my friend Mike bought the Mini Moke, he was going to do it up for his wife Chris. I was going to sail the next day, with Viv taking the plane the following day. We both knew that we were taking a lot more from Nevis, both physically, and spiritually, than what we arrived with. The passage to the anchorage at Marigot was uneventful, we anchored, and came ashore in the dinghy, I treated the skipper to a hearty breakfast and a couple of beers in a harbour-side restaurant as payment for my passage, he was planning on staying in Marigot for the next three or four days, so that was no urgency for me to bring my baggage ashore. He was quite happy to hold onto it until we found suitable accommodation, I really appreciated of the gesture. I set off to Phillipsburg to find the location of the shipping warehouse where our crate had been delivered to. With this done, I had a few hours to spare before Viv was due in, so I took the opportunity of looking round to see what accommodation was available. During the time we were packing I came across the business card of the gentleman from St Maarten to whom we had given half a dozen bags of mangoes. I had his card with me, so just out of curiosity I called him, he was very surprised to hear from me, and even more surprised when I told him that, 'I am at the airport waiting for Viv to land.' He asked me, 'What time is her flight due in?' When I told him, he said that he would be there to pick us up within the hour. As St Maarten benefits from its status as, a 'Duty Free' port there are no customs procedures to follow, and as Viv had bought a return ticket, so there was no issue with immigration. While we were waiting at the airport I picked up a local newspaper and I was busy scouring the classifieds when a gentleman tapped me on the shoulder, he said, 'Hello there I'm the mango man.' We had a cup of coffee and I told them what our plans were. We followed him out to the car park. Viv got into the back seat with the cat, I rode up front with Leonard, he took us to a small hotel on the main street of Phillipsburg, and told as we could stay there until we found suitable accommodation. The place was a bit on the sleazy side, but at least it was free, it belonged to a good friend of his. We were very keen to sort out our own accommodation needs, this happened very quickly and we were able to find temporary accommodation the next day, although it was a little bit primitive – it had a bedroom, a bathroom, and a living room that was miraculously transformed into a dining-room-cum-kitchen. Once we had taken delivery of our packing crate/table, with the addition of a kettle and a single ring electric heater, we had a working kitchen. We were living like teenage students, the cat was getting fed better than we were. I made a call to my contact in Montreal to let him know that I was now in St Maarten and I was now awaiting his instructions as to how I was to proceed in procuring the properties that they required. Unknown to me, the previous week there had been a change of government on the Dutch side of the island, and as a consequence all construction contracts had been cancelled due to contractual irregularities, and all of the containers of equipment and materials that had been transported from Nevis had been seized. This project was not going to start any time in the near future, or it was not going to start at all, that rosy future we were hoping for was suddenly, not looking very rosy after all. Here we go again, almost penniless, almost homeless, in another foreign country.

We met up with a couple of young Brits, David and Peter, they had come to St Maarten with their mother, these two boys were working for a private charter company that owned four racing yachts. These vessels were all ex-America's Cup competition yachts, and the parent company was providing cruise ship passengers with an America's Cup experience. They took me aboard one of their vessels for a sail. I was offered a job but it only paid beer money, not exactly what I was looking for. On a positive side the brothers were renting a house in Simpson Bay, and they offered Viv and I our own bedroom, bathroom, and a shared living room, as well as a fully fitted kitchen. This was a big improvement on our current accommodation so without any hesitation we accepted their offer and moved in right away. Peter had a girlfriend whose name was Erica, she was British, and she had come to the island with her parents, Colm and Shelly. Colm, was in the hospitality industry, he was the Director of Human Resources for the Sheraton resort at Port De Plaisance. He was also a keen sailor, he had his yacht shipped over to the Caribbean and was now in the marina at St Maarten. I was recommended to him by the two boys. Colm wanted some maintenance work doing on his boat, he gave me the job of looking after his boat, we became friends. Colm invited Vivien and I to a barbecue at his home, there we met his wife Shelley. During a conversation with Shelley, she asked Viv if she was looking for a job. Viv said, 'Yes, certainly.' Shelley arranged an interview for Vivien with Marjan Pinczowski. Marjan was married to Ed, the general manager of the Sheraton resort, they were looking for a full-time housekeeper for their home in Simpson Bay. Vivien must have impressed them as she started work immediately. David and Peter turned out to be really useful people to know, they introduced me to another couple, Jacques and Marjella, who owned the restaurant on Simpson Bay beach. They also needed some help with the renovations of an old house that eventually they intended to buy –this was not too far from where their restaurant was located, it was a big house, and quite a renovation project. There was also a self-contained apartment. The apartment was ours for as long as I was working there for them. This worked fine – the apartment was also not too far for Viv to get to her work, things were starting to look up.

Alongside at Wadebridge

Set for dinner

High and dry Wadebridge

Two contenders for figurehead

Leaving Wadesbrige
on River Camel

Following in the wake
of Pliedies

Jock & I on lookout

Safely alongside in Padstow

Home
port of
Charletown

Fore deck crew making ready to cast off

Me at the helm

Leaving Charlestown harbour

St. Austel bay with graham the harbour master

The mate working aloft

Christopher promoted
to forehand

Square sails set

Crewmember on dolphin watch

More sails

Had to shorten the sail

Blue water sailing at its best

Christmas day

The motley crew

A very comfortable cat

Our house and limo

BBQ good friends Nevis

This is a des res with bathroom extension

Viv's promotion four season Nevis

Great friends
from Nevis

Viv and I at the international departure lounge

Viv's team make her farewell banner

Swimming lessons with Alex and Sascha

Viv with Alex and Sascha

My beautiful Dutch angel Sascha

Viv with Alexander

Marjan Viv's boss

Viv in paradise

Christian Bruel serious fishing

Beach Comber villas our home

Me and two helpers getting supper

Getting ready for hurricane louis

Viv looking for our roof

The big clear up

Part of the aftermath

Salvage ship in the background full of wrecks

We rebuild the apartments

Viv on the beach

The author

22

During the renovation there were lots of stripping out to do, old units, cupboards, bathrooms, older dry linings, tiles stripping off walls, old floor coverings – we had the use of a pickup truck which came in very handy for transporting all of the rubbish to the municipal dump. My first visit to the dump was an eye-opener, part of it looked like a scene from Dante's Inferno, there were countless fires burning, giving off acrid smoke, there were also dozens of heaps of smouldering garbage, the atmosphere stung my eyes and hurt the back of my throat. Jacques was driving, when he stopped the truck I reached for the door handle to get out to unload the rubbish but he stopped me. Out of the smoke about 25 to 30 people materialised, they appeared from nowhere and started to swarm all over the back of the truck. He told me that they were salvaging anything that they thought would be useful. 'Where did they come from?' I asked. He pointed to the windscreen, and said 'look' – every now and then a slight breeze would disturb the smoke and through the haze you could just make out half a dozen shacks, or something that resembled a shack. These people were scavenging, they lived on the dump, amidst all this garbage, that was surrounded by clouds of toxic filth. What a wakeup call this was, even on my blackest day, I was never reduced to this level. The truck was emptied in record time, and this scenario is played out every time we had rubbish to dump. After seeing these people living like this I realised just how blessed I have been.

Christopher completed his service with the Royal Navy and decided that he would like to come out to St Maarten with his new girlfriend. They were of the opinion that they would try to find work and maybe even settle here. Christopher came out with me on a few jobs around the Oyster Pond area but this kind of work didn't really appeal to him, so they both went to work for one of the timeshare organisations. I don't think they were very happy with the working conditions and the uncertainty of no work permits. I think this situation started to put pressure on their relationship, and the end product was they separated and Christopher went back to the UK and joined the police force.

Vivien's standard of housekeeping scored very well with Ed and Marjan. The house was rented through a management company they were responsible for minor repairs, and pool maintenance. I ended up looking after the house and the pool. I also ended up looking after some of the properties that the other hotel executives occupied. There was a couple that just live round the corner from Ed and Marjan, Dirk and Suzann. Dirk was a Dutch national, and he was a manager at the airport for KLM, his wife Suzanne, was the daughter of a retired local Government Minister, Mr Julian Connor. Mr and Mrs Connor lived in a beautiful villa at Beacon Hill, just behind the airport, it had a stunning veranda, overlooking the pool deck, that ran down to the beautiful beach at Burgeaux Bay. On the other side of this bay, the Connors owned four apartment buildings. There were ten apartments, mostly used as holiday lets – one or two of the apartments where rented on a permanent basis to tenants who were working on the island. When Mr Connor was away his daughter Suzanne looked after the rental business – she would occasionally use me for any little handyman jobs that needed doing. As Viv was now working full-time and I was also finding plenty of odd jobs, we were also able to rent a nice self-contained apartment in Cole Bay. I also met another expat Brit, his name was Ray, he had a small engineering firm called Momec of Cole Bay. He was very instrumental in me getting established as a handyman. I made a wish list of a good selection of tools that I would need, he placed an order with one of his contacts in the US Virgin Islands, a few days later it felt like Christmas I was presented with a huge selection of tools. When I asked him how much all this would cost me, he said, 'You can repay me when you're back on your feet.' Ray called another friend of his who was in the real estate business, this guy was called Peyton, he was on the French side of the island at a place called Oyster Pond. Ray arranged for me to meet him at his office, this caught me a little by surprise, due to the fact that Oyster Pond was at the far end of the island. Before I could say, 'How do I get there?' he gave me the keys to his pickup, and said, 'You can borrow this until you can afford your own truck.' Peter and James were not that bothered or surprised when we told them that we had found a new apartment, they even helped us move some of our belongings. Peter told me that he had met another sailor that was living on his boat which was anchored in Simpson Bay Lagoon, he was a Scot. Peter gave me directions as to the location of this boat. I was not surprised when I found out that the owner was none other than my old mate Jock. I left a message for him telling him where our apartment was. He turned up about three hours later, we had a good chat and he was horrified when he learnt the fate of *Hafan-y-Mor*. He was telling me that he was doing some delivery work for one of the charter companies 'Sun sail' this involved him taking a boat from St Maarten to Tortola and then he would then bring another boat to St Maarten from Tortola for maintenance. It was a two day round-trip, he asked me about helping him with a few of the deliveries – it wasn't too difficult Viv was quite comfortable in the apartment when I was away for one or two nights. I made about half a dozen trips with him. Mr and Mrs Connor, like most of the other wealthy islanders, would leave the island during the height of the summer for four or five months – this vacation also included being away during the hurricane season. We had a meeting with Mr and Mrs Connor, they asked us to move into their house for the duration of their next holiday. This would involve us living in, and looking after their property for five months. This was a real no-brainier, no rent or utilities to pay for six months and we get to live in a palace, and all we have to do is keep it clean. As the Connors moved out, we moved in – this was island life as it should be, living in a beautiful home, with a stunning pool, and the Caribbean Sea at the bottom of the garden. It didn't take Jock long to find me, he was mightily impressed with my new surroundings and he said that he had an interesting proposition for me, it was for another delivery with the same company, only this time it was a little bit further than Tortola. These two boats had to be delivered to Great Abaco in the Bahamas – in theory it was a two-man crew, in practice, we would take one boat in tow, which meant, that the boat being towed would be left unmanned. This system allowed both crewmen to be on one boat, which meant there would always be at least one crewman awake. We discussed the plan at length, there were many pitfalls, and the main stumbling block again would be Viv being left at home alone for the duration of the trip. But she said it felt more comfortable now, also she felt very safe and secure in the big house. Also she had a good circle of friends and a very good working relationship with Marjan, so we decided that I would join Jock for this passage, and that the money would be useful, and we could put it towards the cost of buying a car. We had a couple of weeks to get Viv settled the into the big house then we had a tentative date to leave it up on what stores that thought we would need. We could not put an exact time frame, there were too many variables to take into account. The estimated around 24–25 days we set off and set up the tow line. We were using about 250 foot tow line, seemed okay, plenty of sea room, we got into a steady rhythm of watch keeping. After about three days at sea, in the vicinity of the Mona Passage, I came across an American aircraft carrier. It was gigantic. I received a message from the carrier on the VHF, instructing me to alter course as they had aircraft about to land, I called the carrier back and advised the radio operator that the rules of the road are quite explicit, and pointed out to him that this was a sailing vessel, currently engaged in the operation of towing, which has reduced my ability to manoeuvre, therefore I have the right-of-way and in order to avoid a collision you must alter course. The operator started to stutter and mumble incoherently. I don't think American warships take it too kindly when they find themselves in a confrontational situation with a tiny sailboat – when I was in Chicago a very charming lady described me as an English gentleman, so be it. I call the radio operator back and told him that, 'I would be prepared to alter course on the condition that you gave me an up-to-date weather forecast.' 'Thank you sir,' came the instant reply, 'please hold while I try to locate our weather officer.' Five minutes later the duty weather officer gave me his forecast – it was a beautiful clear day, he said to me, 'What you see is what you get, it is going to be like this for the next two or three days.' I thanked him and wished him bon voyage. About six hours later we were in the mother of a storm, big seas, big waves, the mast height of the boat were about 45 ft high, there were times when the first 10 ft of the tow rope disappeared into the following wave and we could not see the boat we were towing. On one occasion, the towed vessel came surfing down the wave and overtook our boat, it missed us by about 30 ft. I called Jock and told him I was getting ready to cut the tow adrift, I didn't fancy it crashing through our stern rail. Jock fired the engine up and put a bit of space between us and the towed vessel, it was a bit scary. The rest of the voyage was uneventful, it felt good to be back alongside again. There were a couple of issues with one of the vessels that was being returned to St Maarten, this resulted in us delaying our departure – there was absolutely nothing we could do, it was out of our hands we just had to wait until the vessel was ready. That one day's delay somehow morphed into a week. Fortunately I was able to keep in touch with Viv and give an up-to-date progress report on our lack of progress. The Bahamas are a chain of beautiful islands with pristine beaches, but you can't enjoy something if you don't want to be there. I was impatient to get underway and head back to St Maarten. When both the vessels were ready for sea, and we had an additional two hands for the second vessel, the management thought it was unsafe to return to St Maarten the same way we arrived. Half a day out Jock decided that it was of no benefit to us to have two crew on each boat, it was decided we should tow one boat, and have a crew of four on the boat that was doing the towing, just in case we encountered any more adverse weather on the return journey.

23

The return voyage was uneventful. It was a good day when we made landfall at St Maarten, albeit about 10 days later than anticipated. While we were at sea Viv had no way of contacting us, the only information she could get was from the offices of the chartering company in Phillipsburg, and unfortunately they had very little information, only able to confirm the day and date we left. During this period she did have to consult a doctor, unfortunately she had an adverse reaction to the medication that he had prescribed, she was quite unwell. She was able to get a message to Marjan, who immediately drove to the Connor's house and took Viv back to her house, then called the doctor. Luckily the doctor recognised there had been an error with the dose of the medication that he had prescribed. Vivien stayed with Marjan until I was back home. I made the decision that I would not undertake any more jobs that necessitated me being away from home. During our time at the Connor's house I became more involved with their rental apartments, due to the intransigent nature of a lot of the visitors to St Maarten, many of them would be working without work permits, if and when people were apprehended by the authorities, they would be arrested as illegal immigrants. They would be locked up until they can provide the means of getting back to their home countries, that usually came in the form of an aeroplane ticket, as most of them were usually Americans, they normally came by boat, and they didn't need passports – a driver's licence was sufficient for ID purposes, and most of them did not have access to the funds that would purchase an aeroplane ticket back to mainland USA. So the consequences of being an illegal immigrant meant that a few tenants inadvertently terminated their tenancies. I would have to gain entry, remove personal belongings, and redecorate the apartment for new tenants. When Mr and Mrs Connor returned they were very impressed with the way we looked after their property; their daughter, Suzanne told her parents that I've been very helpful with the Beachcomber apartments.

Mr Connor offered me the position of manager of the apartments, and, as part of the deal we got to live in one of them, and more importantly he assured me that he would have no difficulty in getting Vivien and I work permits.

One of the positive benefits of living in an apartment that is situated on the beach is that you don't have to go very far for a swim. I had never considered myself a strong swimmer but I thoroughly enjoyed snorkelling, it was not unusual for me to take a dip, head down, and kick those fins like they were a little outboard motor. I spent too much time concentrating on what was beneath me, when I stopped to tread water and look around I was horrified at just how far away the beach was. I did not panic, head down again and headed back towards the beach, I was very relieved when I was able to stand up. One Sunday afternoon, one of the young ladies that rented one of the apartments knocked on my door and asked me if she could borrow a saw. I asked her, 'What type of saw do you need?' She sent her boyfriend Jacques to explain, he didn't speak much English, when I asked him what he wanted to cut, he said 'the fish.' I was intrigued. 'Please show me,' I said. he walked down the beach and showed me a shark lying on the sand. I picked it up with both hands just below the tail fin, with its head still on the sand the tail fin was held above my head – it must have been over 6 ft in length. I asked Florence to ask him, 'where did you catch that?' Florence replied, 'About 25 m out from the waterline.' I said to him, 'I swim there every day.' He laughed, 'Don't worry it's only a baby shark, you would be more worried if it's mother came looking for it.' He duly cut the shark up into fillets and he gave me one, it was still pulsating, it put me off fish for a while. I couldn't eat that.

As I started to do more work for Ed and Marjan we got more and more involved with the family, they had two children, Alex and Sascha, we became very close. We would babysit with the children when the parents were busy. It was not unusual for me to do a school run after I dropped Viv off for work. There were also times when we would actually stay over at their house when the parents were away – we were treated like family, not as employees, we had a real good relationship and it was a pleasure to go to work for them, we have such fond memories, We would take the children swimming, where I took the opportunity to try and give Viv some swimming lessons. That did not end well, in a moment of blind panic, the resulting lash out caused me a broken nose, both the children and Viv were quite amused at the sight of me coughing, spluttering, and spitting out snot and blood.

There was a Christmas fair for the children at the school that Alexander and Sascha attended, not exactly sure how it came about, but I ended up making an appearance as Sinterklaas. I was supposed to hop on a helicopter, fly over the hill, then land in the garden. There was an incident, someone was badly injured by the rotor blade, so I was driven in, in the back of a 4x4, the presents were duly handed out, the children were all very happy, especially Alex when he recognised Sinterklass as a friend of his. I can recall Vivien's birthday, the children gave her vouchers for a pampering visit to a real upmarket beauty salon and the children's grandfather, Opah, bought her a Nintendo Game Boy, and Marjan gave her two return airline tickets to the UK, with a week's stay at the Sheraton Hotel Hyde Park London – now that was a birthday she will remember for ever. We made a couple of calls to the UK, then made plans for our holiday, we would arrive in London, stay for a couple nights at the hotel, catch a train down to Brighton to visit Viv's Sister, then we would all drive up to North Wales, spend a week there visiting family, then back to the hotel for a couple of days, get the train to Heathrow, and it was back to the Caribbean. That sounded like a plan, we were able to find a cattery on the French side so even the cat got a holiday. It took a couple of weeks for me to tie up all loose ends, make sure there was nothing outstanding work-wise and all we had to do was pick a date. Our friends, Colm and Shelley asked me would I mind taking some cigarettes to the UK for Erica their daughter, as she was a student. St Maarten was a duty-free port, so cigarettes were very cheap. They gave me a bag with a lot of cigarettes in it, as Viv and I are both non-smokers it didn't matter, or so we thought. When we got to the customs in the UK, because of the quantity I was carrying, I was told I must pay the duty or they would be confiscated. It cost me over a hundred pounds for the privilege of doing somebody a favour. I didn't have the heart to tell Colm, when I returned. We had a good holiday, it was great being able to get round and visit everybody, all of Viv's family were happy to see us together. I think they were disappointed when the time come for us to return, one or two of them secretly hoped that we would decide to stay. I must admit, we gave it some serious thought, but it really did make sense to head back to the Caribbean and see if we could make a go of it. Work was going very well, we even managed to buy a small van, I had quite a string of contacts now, one in particular was Helen Grove, she was a Dutch national who ran a real estate company, she had quite a portfolio of rental properties that needed ongoing maintenance. I hired a couple of local lads, Oscar, he was from Jamaica, and Manno, he was a Haitian. I also took on some work from a couple of private villa rentals, one at Pelican Quay, and the other at Beachside villas, at Beacon Hill. We were approached by a South African lady, Wendy, she had heard we done an excellent job looking after the Connor's household and she wanted to know would we like to look after her house while she was away on holiday for one month, we did not have to live in at the property so that still left Viv with the opportunity to continue working for Marjan. The only downside with this job was that we were expected to do a bit of nanny sitting. Wendy's mother, Nona, would not be going on holiday with them. Nona was quite happy, and able to look after herself, our remit was to see she had a cooked meal a day, and to see that she was able to pop down to the local shops as and when necessary – a car was provided for this service. She was capable of providing her own breakfast, so during the week we would have dinner with her. My job allowed me the flexibility to drive her into town as and when required, we would also spend the weekend at their house. Wendy's husband, George, had a small powerboat on a trailer in his front garden, I spent a couple of hours tidying up and cleaning it, and I undertook a few maintenance tasks in and around the house. While we were in Okehampton, Viv owned a motorcycle that she used for getting to and from work, I was not very keen on the idea of Viv riding around the country lanes of Devon on a motorcycle, and I persuaded her to consider the possibility of taking driving lessons so she could eventually drive a car. This she done for six months, but as the boat project started, she decided to discontinue the lessons. She had taken more lessons from the police driving instructor on Nevis. St Maarten had no driving test facility, so if you wanted to drive, you did, all you needed was a car, she took to island driving like a duck to water. I took every opportunity to let her drive the car as and when she needed it. I was always in the car with her, but after two weeks she was comfortable driving the car by herself, she was very pleased with herself when she would turn up for work and ask Marjan, 'Is there anything you need from the shops?' The four-week nanny and house sitting came to an end, with Viv feeling quite disappointed at the loss of her newly acquired independence. I used the money we earned from the housesit to buy Viv her own little car, my friend Ray, the engineer found, and serviced a suitable Daihatsu compact runabout – he sorted out mechanical side, while I did the valeting, I tied a pink ribbon around it, and parked it behind his workshop. I went to pick Viv up after she finished work, we drove down to the main road, we normally turn left to head off to Beacon Hill, as we turned right, she said, 'Where are we going?' I said quizzically, 'Just a minor detour, as you have to pick something up from Ray's workshop.' 'Really?' she said, 'What's the possibility of Ray having anything that I would need to pick up?' She was quite concerned as I drove past the front entrance to Ray's workshop. As we drove round to the back of the workshop, she saw the car with the ribbon tied around it. It didn't really register, until I asked her to get out of the van, and I presented her with her car keys – she was overjoyed.

24

Wendy came to see me and told me that her husband George was quite impressed by the way we looked after is house, his boat, and his mother-in-law, and that he wanted to see me with a view to doing some work in the casino that he managed in Phillipsburg. I went along to the casino and asked the concierge, 'Could I speak to the manager, George please?' He shrugged and said, 'You mean Giorgio?' 'If he's the manager yes.' He asked for my name, went into his office and picked up the phone. He rattled off a set of questions in Italian, that finished with 'Mike Nolan to see you'. He led me through the casino to the manager's office and knocked on the door. Another voice was asking him questions in Italian, The door was opened, I was led into a very sumptuous office and told to wait, the manager will be with you shortly. Two gentlemen came into the office, one of them introduced himself as Giorgio, he was very Italian, he thanked me profusely for the work done at his home and the asked me if I could do some work in the cashier's office. His associate took me to the office and explained to me what he wanted doing, then asked if I could do it. I said, 'yes' it was nothing too technical just fitting new armoured Perspex screens, I was told to proceed with the job and submit my bill on completion. This I did. The other gentleman was quite satisfied with the standard of work, and he didn't question the bill I presented. Viv and I were invited to George and Wendy's house for dinner, George spoke passable English, with Wendy on hand to clarify anything lost in translation. He said, 'Wendy has told me that you are a boat man.', 'Yes sailboat,' I said. He told me that the casino owned a boat that was used for entertaining their guests, and would I be interested in looking after it? I would be paid for my time, and for any maintenance that I undertook, as well as being paid for any time that I used the boat for their guests. The downside was I had to be available to drive the boat as and when it was needed, the upside was I would always be given notice at least a couple of days' notice, to make sure the boat was fully fuelled before the boat was due to be used. The icing on the cake was, if the boat was not needed, I could have it for my own personal use. I agreed terms, we shook hands on it, he gave me a set of keys, and told me that the boat was currently moored in the Marigot marina on the French side and that he would like it to be moored on the Dutch side by the airport. He told me that it had a red and black hull, and gave me the pontoon number that it was alongside. There was no time frame but I told them I would check it out at the coming weekend. The following Sunday we drove over to the French side to find this boat – what a shock when I saw it, it was very sleek, about 30 ft in length, with a centre steering console, very plush seating for at least 12 passengers, and it was powered by twin, 230 HP outboard engines. I couldn't begin to imagine what sort of speed this boat would reach, and to be honest it frightened me to death. I passed my concerns to Wendy, she told me she'd have a chat with George, and his reaction was, 'You must know what you are doing, you sailed your boat across the Atlantic Ocean.' I took it for a spin around the lagoon then out into Simpson Bay, then back to its new berth, I was not impressed, this was a high-speed motorboat that would have been more at home on the set of *Miami Vice*. Ed and Marjan's contract was coming to an end, they were getting ready to relocate to Antalya in Turkey. We would miss the family terribly, we had grown quite close to them, especially the children, Alexander and Sasha. We were on hand to help the packing, and there were many tears when the leaving date arrived. Ed was leaving the Sheraton on Saint Maarten to manage the Sheraton in Antalya Turkey and the general manager from Antalya was coming to take over from Ed. The new manager, Christian Bruel, and his wife Merete were Danish. Christian had worked for the Sheraton for many years. Acting on the references from Ed and Marjan Pinckowski, Christian and Merete continued to employ Vivien as their housekeeper, I also fell back into the position of handyman. As with the previous tenants, both Vivien and I got on very well with Christian and Merete, we soon became friends. Christian told me that he liked to do some sea fishing, I just let it slip that I had access to a boat that I could use, I did specify that it was not exactly a fishing boat, he was of the opinion that if it floated it was a boat. I told him to check his calendar and let me know when he had a free day and I would provide the boat, he was intrigued, and hooked. A couple of days later Christian called me and said that he would be free that weekend. I arranged to pick him and his fishing rods up at about eight o'clock. As we were walking down the dock we came to the boat, and he was just a tiny bit surprised. His reaction was 'I've never been out fishing on a drug runner's boat.' We drove it out of the lagoon, and had a very pleasant cruise around the island, with Christian catching the fish. I wasn't very comfortable with the responsibility of this boat and its passengers, fortunately for me that problem was resolved immediately. I was introduced to Terry, he was South African, living on his boat with his wife and two sons, he was also the captain of one of the big day charter sail boats, he was more than happy to come out with us on the casino boat. A couple of weeks later we took Christian, and some of his friends out for a nice picnic to Île Tintamarre, one of the smaller islands, and caught a few fish on the return trip, a good day was had by all. I got a call from George telling me that the boat would be needed for four guests and would I meet them at the pontoon at eight o'clock in the morning. I made sure the boat was pristine, fully fuelled and ready to go. I met the guests. There were two couples, the two ladies were definitely contenders for the Miss Universe contest, the gentleman, clean cut well-dressed businessmen, I had a cold box with drinks and snacks if needed. They wanted to go to Anguilla, which was only nine miles away. I asked them if they wanted to go to Blowing Point Port, they said that we would like to go round to the other side of the island, to Crocus Bay. 'There are no docking facilities at Crocus Bay,' I said. 'Oh that's no problem you can just run up onto the sand,' was the curt reply. An hour later we slid slowly onto the sandy beach. 'We will be having breakfast ashore so we should be back in about two hours.' One of the gentleman was carrying an aluminium briefcase, they returned two hours later, empty-handed. I sailed them back to the pontoon, they left and I was back home just after midday, I did not do that trip again, I was not very confident , and I was a little bit unsure of exactly what the nature of the trip was. The passengers were not very talkative, Terry was quite happy to continue looking after the casino boat.

Vivien thought it would be a good time for her to go back to the UK to visit her family, hopefully this time would be no passport issues. We had already flown to Florida for a holiday, that we thoroughly enjoyed, and there was no immigration issues as we both had individual passports. Viv went on her holiday back to the UK to visit her family, she went on her own because I was very busy, this year's hurricane season looked like it was going to be very active – if the predictions were correct I was going to be very busy. Hurricane Iris, came and went without too much trouble. As normal when Viv returned from the UK she was laden down with Walls finest. The long-range forecast picked up a storm coming off Cape Verde, I was following it on my tracking chart when it was later upgraded to a hurricane, and judging by the course it was following alarm bells started to ring. Most of the larger houses that I was looking after all had built-in shutters, so it was quite a straightforward operation to secure them, the buildings at beachcomber villas had no protection, so I made shutters out of plywood sheets for the four apartments in my building, then spent the day cutting them and securing them. We took all the necessary precautions, stocked up on water and waited for the storm. My building had four apartments, two had been vacated, along with the rest of the apartment buildings. Paul and Kylie were the young couple that stayed in the apartment above ours – they couldn't leave as they had three dogs, not exactly sure of the day and the date but it was around fifth or sixth of September 1995.

25

St Maarten has a huge inland lagoon that is considered to be the safest hurricane hole in the Caribbean. A couple of days before this my friend Jock and I secured his boat, then we proceeded to secure Johan's boat. We laid an extra couple of anchors, and also secured it to a couple of palm trees that were close to the shore, we were of the opinion that this boat could end up in trouble just because of the size of the cabins it would create a lot of windage, we did our best. Jock said that he wouldn't be staying aboard his boat. I asked him if he wanted to come to our apartment, he said, 'No thanks I have got some accommodation fixed up in Cole Bay.' On my way back to Beacon Hill, I did a quick check on the other properties that I secured, all that could be done, had been done. I went home to join Viv and the cat. The wind was getting stronger, and noisier, with the addition of driving rain. The noise was almost unbearable, we were very surprised and frightened at the apparent ease of the way the plywood sheets, that had been bolted to the wall, where ripped off the window frames and left us to the mercy of the waves. Every other panel of the window glass was fitted with small shutters that opened, they were also ripped out. Fortunately the side of the house that was overlooking the sea had a wooden floor so I was able to smash some of the floorboards, and allow all of the water to drain away, judging by the amount of water that was coming through the ceiling it was safe to assume that Paul and Kylie in the apartment above us, had lost the roof. The apartments had a stairwell, this allowed the sea spray, the wind, the rain, and any other debris that were picked up off the beach to be funnelled through the opening like an express train, the sea water would pour through the gaps in the doorjambs, as if somebody was on the outside using a pressure hose. Rocks the size of footballs were hurled against the side of the house, miraculously none of them hit the windows, it must be a very similar feeling of being in a building that is being attacked by cannon fire. Beacon Hill Road runs out to create a peninsular, on the far side was Simpson Bay Lagoon, at this end of Simpson Bay there was no beach just rocks with the cliff face about 20 ft high, every so often a huge wave would smash into this cliff and the whole of the surrounding area vibrated. We thought the building might collapse. This didn't do Viv's nervous disposition any good at all. As daybreak came, the wind abated, it was very surreal, we knew this was the eye wall of the storm and this was just a small break before we went into round two. We had prepared a few sandwiches and a couple of bottles of water, so we took advantage of the low winds and lack of noise to grab some breakfast. I couldn't open the door to check what it was like outside, we were trapped, we couldn't get out if we wanted to. I was able to contact Paul by shouting up through the ceiling, he confirmed my suspicion about the roof, and he also told me that lost a couple of the windows. The way the building was constructed probably saved our lives – one half of the building was of a concrete construction, a small kitchen, bathroom, and two bedrooms. We had put a mattress inside the bathroom and that's where we stayed, as did Paul and Kylie upstairs, along with the three dogs. As the eye of the storm passed over and the wind started to pick up again, we retreated back to the safety of the bathroom and waited for the inevitable.

Hurricane Luis, was a category five storm, with sustained winds of about 130 mph, and recorded gusts of over 200 mph, the eye was about 40 mile in diameter with peripheral winds of about 200 miles either side, it slowed down to about 8 mph, and it took over 36 hours for the storm to pass.

We had to endure another 14 or so hours of confinement in the bathroom while we listened to the storm raging outside, when it was all over, I still could not open the door to get out. I was able to climb out through the window and went through to the stairwell, there I was confronted with what was left of the staircase. I had the foresight to turn off and disconnect the four LPG bottles, lay them down and chain them to one of the newel posts, everything was a mess with dozens of palm fronds, and a few tons of sand and stone.

I had chained my ladders to the small wall at the front of the house, so I was able to let Paul and Kylie, along with their very happy dogs, out to get some fresh air. When we surveyed the damage to some of the properties in our immediate vicinity it became very obvious to us that we were very fortunate to have survived this nightmare, one of the houses on the beach had completely disappeared. We started to clear up our immediate surround-ings and make what emergency repairs we could. We walked up to the side of the cliff that overlooks Simpson Bay, immediately to the left I could see beachside villas – before the storm there were 14 villas on the beach, seven of them had disappeared completely, there appeared to be only one of them left habitable, the rest were in dire need of major repair work. Apparently this was the norm for most of the homes on the island. The airport was closed, as were both of the major harbours, this did not bode well island dwellers, everything that wasn't ruined was probably looted. Martial law was insti-gated, along with a curfew, the rule was simple – armed soldiers and police to shoot anyone out after dark. St Maarten boasts the safest hurricane hole in the Caribbean, Simpson Bay Lagoon. This is where most of the boats in the eastern Caribbean head to for safety during a hurricane, there were about 1500 vessels of every description anchored in the lagoon, and most of these would be live aboard yachts. After the storm there were less than 300 ves-sels afloat, those that had not sunk had been smashed to pieces, others were stacked randomly on top of each other, even saw some on top of buildings. My friend Terry, who owned a 45 foot sailing boat, could not even find a piece of wreckage big enough so that he could identify it as being part of his boat. The motor yacht that belonged to Johann disappeared completely. The authorities were very vague about casualties.

Due to St Maarten's unique duty-free status there is little or no control over immigration, so it is safe to assume that about 70% of the population are there illegally, so there was no accurate way to measure exactly what a casu-alty list would be. In many of the marinas, bars, and restaurants that were frequented by the yachting fraternity there where many, 'Have you seen' lists – it's safe to assume that if lots of yachts are lost, so would be their crews and owners. The military armed with huge bulldozers just levelled some of the sites where the shanty-towns were, and buried all the debris.

I was contacted by the owner of one of the properties that I had done some work on at beachside villas. We met on site, and went to what was left of one of his villas. We walked through the patio of his villa and into the living room. When I opened the door to the living room I saw that the entire back walls of the building had disappeared, and much to my surprise the floor that I was standing on collapsed. I fell into what looked like a cellar that was filled with building rubble, obviously the storm surge had completely undermined the foundations of the building. I was trapped by the debris, with one piece of rebar, that had punctured my left side just under my armpit, a second piece of rebar had punctured my neck, just under my chin, and I had ripped open the back of my thigh from just behind the knee to my buttock on a piece of jagged floor tile. I was well and truly skewered, it was almost impossible to move, somehow, with the owner's help, I was raised up just enough for me to get a foothold on a block of masonry. I was able to relieve the weight on the two pieces of the rebar that had punctured me, He helped me to climb out of the hole, he patched me up the best he could and then he took me home. Viv was quite concerned, she was of the opinion that I needed to get to the hospital. I was feeling a slightly uncomfortable and in a bit of pain so I went to lie down. Shortly afterwards Viv returned with one of the other tenants that had just come over to check on her apartment, she was a French national who was working in Marigot, she was with a friend of hers, who was a doctor, and currently working at the hospital on the French side. She decided that I needed to be hospitalised. The main roads were now passable but the curfew was still in force, the doctor said we would be all right, we got into the car and set off. We were just coming up to, Les Terres Basses, when we came across a roadblock manned by armed French Marines. I have never been so relieved to be in the company of two French speaking ladies, after the Marines lowered their guns, they allowed the car to pass, they even offered to provide us with an escort to the hospital. I will owe the both of them my everlasting gratitude for the unbelievable care and compassion that was shown to me by those two French ladies. We were allowed to proceed to the hospital where I was treated. They said it would be much safer if I spent the night there. I didn't argue, Viv came and picked me up the next day. I had to take it easy for a day or two. It would be a long time before things got back to normal, there were shortages of everything, all of the shops had been destroyed, or badly damaged, there was no water or electricity, the whole island was in a mess, things were going to get a lot worse.

26

Things started to improve slightly, some of the shops had even managed to get basic provisions on their shelves. I had to queue at the local shop for the bread, if the queues got a bit unruly, and they did, the odd use of a cattle prod here and there brought the queue back to stability.

Just when we all thought that things were getting back to normal, Hurricane Marilyn formed in the Atlantic, and this one was following the same track as the last one. Thankfully it was nowhere as severe as Luis, at least this one brought us lots of rain, so the good news was, that at least it washed all the sand and salt off everything.

We had no water or electricity, all our food was cooked on an open fire on the beach. I suppose it was one up from the beach barbecue. A couple of the houses that I was looking after had swimming pools and cisterns, the cisterns we used to collect and store rainwater, so at least we had access to plenty of fresh water. Being on the boat had taught us to be frugal with fresh water and bathe in the sea – for the toilet, it was back to bucket and chuck it, then we would use freshwater for hair and teeth. We also had the use of a generator, so the fridge and freezer were still working. I would normally ration my supply of Walls finest, but the situation was critical so we had to empty the freezer as soon as we could, so for the next week I had lots of sausages, they went down very well.

One of the positive results of the storm was that now construction workers were in great demand. I had to spend all my time working on Beachcomber villas. I was having to turn down a lot of good paying jobs. My first priority was for Mr Connor's home and our apartment buildings, all of the apartments needed new roofs, and all of the windows replacing as well as decorating inside and out. Mr Connor's house needed work done on the patio and veranda. I had come across a couple of good Canadian carpenters who I sub-contracted this work out to. While we were waiting for all the materials to be shipped in for the renovation of our apartments, I went to work for beachside villas. I was asked to project manage the site, but I had to refuse because I couldn't guarantee them my full-time attention due to my commitment with our own apartments.

I was able to liaise with the new contractor for him to keep my own couple of lads fully employed until I needed them. When all the materials had finally arrived we were working full-time to get the job completed. Once all the renovations on the apartments were done I went back to work for beachside villas.

All of the main construction was done, I was just involved with the fitting out all the kitchens and tiling. It was a very hectic year, all of the family back in the UK where much relieved that we were able to walk away with just a few bruises, and a slight battering. One of Viv's sisters, Avril contacted us and said that an old friend of Vivien's had made contact with he and told her that she had spent a long time trying to find Vivien – this lady was Marjorie Traynor, this was a very good friend from over 30 years ago. She had even resorted to putting an ad in the local rag in the lost and found: this is how Avril found out she was looking for Viv. She was quite keen to get in touch, and she asked Viv, 'Would you mind if I gave her your address.' She did so. After a couple of letters, and half a dozen long distance phone calls she decided that she would like to come and visit us. She was just a little bit surprised to learn of the incredible journey and adventure that brought us to where we were today.

Marjorie stayed with us the two weeks and Vivien thoroughly enjoyed her company, reminiscing about the good old days. Marjorie had a little bit of a problem trying to come to terms with the dramatic transformation that she had seen from Vivien, as a timid shop assistant to the second-in-command of a sailing ship that had sailed across the Atlantic Ocean, and who then survived a shipwreck and three hurricanes. Marjorie was impressed, she enjoyed her stay with us, and it was quite sad when the time came for them to say goodbye.

During this time we had also had to say goodbye to some of the good friends who had to be relocated due to the hotels being closed. Colm, and Shelley went back home to Canada. Colm wanted me to sail his boat over to the United States, this was out of the question, I would have needed at least three months. Fortunately my friend Terry and one of his sons offered to do the job. I put him in touch with Colm, they worked the details out, I just helped with the preparation. Then they set sail for the USA. Christian and Merete transferred to the Sheraton hotel just outside Albufeira in Portugal, we kept in touch. I vaguely remember another threat that came in the shape of tropical storm Sebastien, towards the end of the hurricane season, Christian said to me, 'Don't you think that it's time that you two left the Caribbean?'

Just after Christmas, we decided it was time to move on because we could not face another hurricane season, and we started to make plans. There were no direct flights to the UK, the choice was either Amsterdam, with KLM, or Paris with Air France. Where ever we landed we would still have to get to the UK so we settled on Paris. This presented a problem with the cat because we needed to put the cat in a cattery due to the quarantine rules in the UK, so we decided we could fly into Paris, Viv would sort the cat out and I would sort out the cargo. The first item was the cat, we were able to get the address and location of a decent cattery not too far from the Charles de Gaulle airport in Paris; the second item, what were we going to take with us, luckily I still had my trusty old packing crate, the same rules applied, what did not fit in the case would not be coming with us. We managed to pack the crate, everything else would be the subject of another yard sale. The crate was booked in as cargo, as was the cat. Once all the arrangements had been made to leave St Maarten, we had no plans of exactly of what we would do when we got to Paris. Christian Bruel insisted that we come to Portugal and stay with them to a couple of weeks until we decided exactly where and what we were going to go. So now we had some idea of a plan, once we had landed, Viv would collect the cat, get a taxi to the cattery, then return to the cargo terminal. We would then make our way to the Metro – once in Paris, we would get the Eurostar to London, then onto Brighton where we would be met by Viv's sister and brother-in-law. We also needed to sort out a suitable method of transport, once this was done all we had to do was to drive to the ferry port, then on to Paris. Viv would go off in the taxi again to retrieve the cat, while I was unpacking the crate at the cargo terminal and repacking the car, what possibly go wrong? Now that all the arrangements were in place it was all systems go, we had a farewell barbecue on the beach to say goodbye to everybody, it also doubled up as our yard sale, it all went very well. We vacated our apartment at beachcomber, another good friend of ours, Lilian, allowed us to stay in her villa at Pelican Quay in Simpson Bay for a couple of days until our flight time. On the leaving day she took us to the airport, we waved goodbye to the Caribbean. The flight was uneventful, apart from a six-hour delay spent on the ground at Lille airport, some sort of fuel problem, there was nearly a riot on the plane the gendarmes had to be called to quieten down some unruly French people that were very angry at being stuck on an aeroplane for six hours, we eventually arrived at our destination, albeit six hours late.

Viv had a nightmarish four hour taxi journey, When she returned she was not a happy bunny, she swore that she would ever get into a French taxi ever again. We eventually found ourselves at the Eurostar terminal, where we caught the train to London. Due to the delays we just missed the connection for the Brighton train and we had to take a taxi. We eventually got to Brighton about a day later than we anticipated. We spent a couple of days just relaxing and trying to get back to normal. Dennis had been busy trying to find us a suitable vehicle, he had been able to provide us with a Citroen BX automatic estate, that looked like it would fit the bill, it had a towing hitch so we bought a small trailer. About a week later we set off for the ferry port at Portsmouth, took the ferry to Le Havre, then on to the cargo terminal at the airport. The drive was okay, so we decided that, under great duress, Viv would go by taxi to the Parisian cat house to collect the cat, that would free me up to concentrate all my efforts on loading the car and trailer. I was able to dismantle the crate, then use the timber for boxing in the sides of the trailer, this worked very well. I was just about finished when Viv turned up with the cat. I think it was pleased to see me, Viv was. It had been a long and tiring day so we decided to get clear of Paris and find a small hotel, have something to eat and get an early night so we could be up bright and early in the morning to start our 1000 mile journey.

27

I think it was pleased to see me, Viv was. Our first overnight stop was at Montauban, just north of Toulouse, the following day we set off heading for Bilbao in Spain, and then on to Burgos, this leg of the journey included driving across the Pyrenees, which was as spectacular as it was frightening at the same time – we were driving around hairpin bends with zero visibility because of low clouds. We were very relieved when we started the descent, we got as far as Salamanca before we felt the need to rest for the night. We set off on the last leg crossing the border at Badajoz with our ETA at Albufeira for about three o'clock in the afternoon. When we arrived at Albufeira, we stopped for fuel, and we were able to contact Christian, he gave me directions and instructions for gaining access to the resort.

Pine Cliffs is a beautiful Sheraton resort, set in a truly stunning location. We were directed to the manager's residence – it was a fabulous villa with its own pool and gardens. Christian and Merete, were very pleased to see us and they insisted we stayed there with them until we could find suitable accommodation for ourselves. They had an important conference to attend that necessitated them being away four days, we didn't even have enough time to unpack before they had to leave. He called the executive chef, Christian Hildorf, a fellow Dane, from the hotel kitchens and instructed him to look after us until they returned – what hospitality, we were well and truly spoilt.

When they returned we were able to relax with them and retell all the hurricane tales, and we also gave them an mile by mile description of the ups and downs of the journey from Paris, to Brighton. Then from Brighton to Paris, and on through France Spain and finally Portugal, they were quite amused. We stayed with them for about three weeks, at the end of the last week we had arranged for two of Viv's sisters and their families to join us for a holiday, we rented a really nice villa in Almancil for two weeks. We had a really nice

BBQ and we invited Christian and Merete, as well as Christian Hildorf and his girlfriend Maria. It was just our way of saying thank you to them for all the help we had been given over the past couple of months.

We were able to find a nice apartment in a quaint little fishing village just a few miles east of Albufeira, it was called Olhos de Agua, now all we had to do was find a job. We answered an ad in an English newspaper, the owners of the property were looking for a couple, a housekeeper and handyman. We went to a beautifully, quaint little town called Silves for an interview with a Norwegian gentleman, his name was Erik, he was married with two young children, Eloise and Maud.

He was a financial consultant, their home was a large old stone farmhouse in an olive grove on the mountain, they were in the process of completely renovating another even larger house.

When this was completed the family would then move to the big house, it also included a self-contained annex, which would be our accommodation.

Mr and Mrs Langaker, had employed a young English girl as the nanny for the two young children. She was not very happy with the solitude of living on the mountain, she did not last very long which resulted in a huge change to my duties. I went from handyman to nanny again, fortunately I got on very well with the two children so I didn't consider it too much of an inconvenience when I had to switch from handyman to childminder. We were looking forward to the completion of the renovations on the new property as then we would be on site, the drive to work each day was a little bit tedious – it was about a 45 mile round trip. There was one occasion when I became ill, I was diagnosed with shingles – having this condition, it was not good to be around young children. It was almost impossible for Viv to make her own way to work so she had to stop working until I was fit again, on one occasion, when she was stranded on the N 125 at Guia, we had no telephone at this time, somehow she managed to get a call to Merete who had to come and rescue her. The family went on holiday and during this break I was asked by Mrs Langaker's parents to do some work at their home that was just outside Portimao. It was mainly gardening, and fitting a shelving unit in an oddly shaped storeroom, this did not take very long, so we had a few days to ourselves. When the family returned Eric told me that they would be employing a new nanny, so would I mind concentrating on preparing a couple of rooms for the new nanny in the garage space? he also told me that he was having some issues with a couple of the local politicians about employing non-nationals. Unfortunately, Eric was from Norway, and as such was not a citizen of the EEC – the local politicians, being typical, did not object to a very wealthy individual investing in their community, but they did like to exercise their authority by placing hurdles in his way concerning whom he could employ. It soon became obvious that this was not going to be the secure well paid job that we thought it would be.

When the new nanny arrived we were given two weeks holiday, so we put the cat in the cattery for the two weeks, then took the opportunity to return to the UK for a holiday and explore the possibility of finding employment then relocating back to the UK. If we decided to relocate we would have a major problem in deciding what to do about the cat. It was going to cost a small fortune to fly the cat back to the UK, then into quarantine for the next six months. I promised Viv that if we were able to secure employment we would be in a position to be able to afford all the relevant costs – the alternative was too horrendous to consider, the cat had undoubtedly used up all of its nine lives, surviving the shipwreck, one hurricane at sea, and three hurricanes on land, and as much as it grieves me to admit it, I had grown quite fond of it. We spent the day driving up through Spain to Santander, then caught the ferry to Portsmouth, we decided that this was the least stressful method of travelling back to the UK. Once on board the ferry we were able to relax and enjoy the crossing.

The cabin was very comfortable, there was also a good choice of restaurants, plus entertainment in one of the show bars.

When we docked at Portsmouth it was only a two-hour drive to West Sussex, where we would stay with Viv's sister and her husband Dennis.

We spent the first few days earnestly checking out the job market, preferably we would be looking for a position that provided us with accommodation, that narrowed the field.

There are a good selection of vacancies for domestic positions in the situations vacant section of *The Lady* magazine. We attended a couple of interviews for positions in and around the Brighton area, the one that look most promising was in Hertfordshire – the only downside was it was a box number, in my reply to the ad I made it very clear that will be we would be leaving the UK again in about ten days. I had also given Avril's telephone number as a contact. This worked, I was called by Mr William Noad, after a short conversation he offered us an interview, he suggested that if we came by train to Borehamwood, somebody would be there to pick us up at the station. He gave me the details, and even the time of which train to catch. According to the timetable we would be arriving at Borehamwood at 1400 hrs. we caught the train from Brighton, all went well until we noticed that, as we approached Borehamwood station the train did not slow down, this particular train went directly to London, as we were due to be picked up at the station nobody thought it necessary to give us the address of the property or the contact details. We were able to get the next train back that would be stopping at Borehamwood. Mr Noad's eldest son Thomas, had gone to the station to collect us, he assumed correctly that we were on the train that didn't stop, he spoke to the station master who told him, 'It will be an hour and 15 minutes before any train from London comes back to this station.' Thank heaven for common sense, he came back to the station at 1515 hrs, as we were the only couple that got off the train he came over and introduced himself and took us to his car, he then proceeded to drive us to his home. We were very impressed with the drive, and when we came to the house we were amazed, it was a beautiful period mansion house, due to the close proximity of the Elstree Film Studios, this estate is a very popular location that is used extensively by the film industry. The property was used as a location for some scenes in a Tom Cruise film. Tom Cruise, was very impressed with High Cannons – his then wife, Nicole Kidman, their children, and their entire entourage, took over the whole estate and made it their home for the duration of a complete film that they were both working on. The film was called *Eyes Wide Shut*, this took about seven months I believe.

The interview was successful and we were offered the position. Due to the fact that we were late getting to the interview, as well as spending more time than we should have talking about our escapades, Mr Noad offered to drive us to the station. Just as we were about to get in his car he said, 'I must show the cottage, you will be living in the annexe.' This was a very quaint-looking cottage with a small front garden. Mr Noad knocked on the front door, the current housekeeper and the caretaker were at home and just having their evening meal. It was a little bit awkward being introduced to your replacements, this couple were retiring and had been on the property for many, many years. It all happened too quickly to take it all in, all we could remember was a living room with a fire burning, a small kitchen, bathroom and bedroom, it looked cosy. Mr Noad drove us to the station, we agreed that it would take about a month to sort out everything in Portugal, and as soon as we have a definite leaving date we would notify him.

We took the train back to Brighton, Dennis and Avril were very pleased, as was the rest of Viv's family, now that they all knew that we were coming back to the UK. The last couple of days were spent trying to organise and locate a suitable cattery where the cat could be quarantined. We found one in Hitchin, that was about 25 miles away from High Cannons, we made all the arrangements, then we set off back to Portsmouth to catch the ferry to Spain, then for the final journey back to Olhos de Agua in Portugal.

28

The trip went very well. When we returned to work we had a meeting with Mr and Mrs Langaker, explained our position, then asked them how much notice would they require, they were little bit shocked at our decision, but upon reflection it would be more beneficial to them if they were to employ locals, the last thing they needed were complications with their building plans. We parted on good terms. It was just as well that I kept the packing crate, we were about to use it again, only this time we had a lot more stuff to ship, so this time we did the sensible thing, we contacted a company that provided a courier service for expats who were relocating to the UK. This seemed ideal, we decided to carry the bare minimum in the car, the rest would be collected for delivery to the UK when we had a definite date. We went to say farewell, and thanks to Christian and Merete, we set a date of Monday, 1st December to start work, so we advised Mr Noad. He told me that the family would be away for that weekend but we were more than welcome to come over at any time to get settled in, and that he would leave the keys for the cottage with the residents of the Gatehouse Lodge and we could pick them up there. Also he said that he was 'looking forward to seeing us on the Monday.' We made all the arrangements with the courier, we were going to leave on the 26th of November, they came that day and collected all our belongings, we then set off for the ferry port in Spain.

When we boarded the boat for the journey to Portsmouth, again it was like the last trip, very enjoyable. When we arrived back into the UK we only spent a couple of hours with Avril and Dennis before we set off to High Cannons to begin the next chapter.

We arrived at the Gatehouse, introduced ourselves and collected the keys for the annexe. The driveway was even more impressive than I remembered, as we pulled up outside the annexe, we were now seeing this house in broad daylight. We opened the door and walked into the hall, we were not impressed, we then went into the living room, it was filthy, as was the kitchen, the bathroom and the bedroom. Vivien was horrified, it was a unanimous decision, we would not be staying there, as the owners were away we had no way of contacting them, we went back to the Gatehouse, returned the keys and left Avril's telephone number so Mr Noad would be able to contact us. We told the gatekeeper that we would return on Monday morning. We returned to the annexe at about 07:30 , the family were back in residence. I went over to the big house and asked to see Mr Noad, I told him, that 'we will definitely not be living in that cottage.' He seemed surprised, I asked him, if he had actually seen the inside of the house.? He said, 'Yes, last month when I showed it to you and your wife, it's nice little cottage.' I replied, 'Would you like to come and have a look at it now in daylight?' 'Okay,' he said, 'lead the way.' When we got round to the front of the cottage Viv was still sitting in the car. He said, 'Good morning come on in, and show me what you think the problem is.' In the cold light of day he conceded that the current condition of the cottage was not suitable for habitation. He asked me, 'How long would it take for me to make it habitable?' I replied, 'Three to four weeks.' He said that the estate would provide me with all the materials I needed to complete the renovation, and there was a self-contained apartment that we could use until the cottage was ready. That was an acceptable solution that both Viv and I agreed to, she went to start work as the housekeeper, I started the renovations on the cottage, the priority was bedroom first, bathroom, then kitchen. The whole project took me about three weeks, the owners were very pleased with the results, as was Viv. The only downside was that during the first week, I received a telephone call from the courier informing me that his vehicle and driver had been involved in a nasty collision that resulted in the entire contents of his vehicle, including our belongings, being spread out along 300 yards of the A62, just south-west of Burgos in southern Spain. It later transpired that the driver and his vehicle were not insured. There are times like this when you do some deep soul searching try and figure out if you had been a bad guy in a previous life.

As we got more settled we decided it was time to go and collect the cat from the quarantine kennel. We picked the cat up and got into the car. Vivien had the cat sitting on her lap, the first thing that the cat did was to raise her back and pee all over Vivien. She was not amused, I personally thought it was hilarious. Vivien actually encouraged me to ignore the current speed regulations and get home as soon as possible. As we got more settled in to the new house, we were able to get into the routine of the household. Mr Noad was in the legal profession working in London, his wife Siri, was from Norway, they had two sons, Thomas and David, they both attended Harrow. As was the norm we got on very well with the family. Thomas went up to Cambridge, David and I helped him move his belongings to his accommodation. While they were both together as Harrow, Thomas was very interested in performing arts and theatre production. For the end of term concert, they put on a play by Terence Rattigan, *The Winslow Boy*. There was a slight difference between this and the normal school play, the pupils directed and produced the play, the actors were parents of the pupils, the cast was made up from some seriously famous names – the only one I can definitely recall was Peter O'Toole, his son Lorcan was in the same class as David. He came to High Cannons for afternoon tea to discuss the play with Thomas and David. Vivien was quite taken aback when she had to make scones and tea for Peter O'Toole. The house was used quite often by various film crews – if the family were away, or on holiday, I would liaise with the location manager to make sure they only went where they were supposed to go, needless to say I was on very good terms with all of the production staff. It was quite interesting to be on the inside watching how some of the scenes were set and what the final outcome was. We were taking a more proactive approach to the work we were doing and getting more involved with the family, especially if it came to entertaining. Normally Mrs Noad would prepare the food and Vivien and I would serve then clear up. Then we got more involved in the preparation and making the food as well as serving it, so it was not unusual to find ourselves working longer hours, but we enjoyed it.

I have a sister Valerie, she lives in County Mayo Ireland, she told me that my brother Thomas was seriously ill in hospital with kidney failure. He was having dialysis at their unit in Leicester when a donated kidney became available, as he was already at the hospital he was partially prepared. He was taken to the theatre to prepare him for the transplant, the second recipient on the waiting list did not turn up, the surgeons, not wanting to waste a viable kidney, gave both of them to Thomas, a bilateral transplant, when we went to see him he told me it was like winning the lottery – it was good being back in contact with Thomas and Marlene. We went to see him a couple of times while he was at the hospital, when the transplant team were happy with his progress he was discharged, they were living in Cranwell just outside Sleaford in Lincolnshire. Cranwell is also the home of the world- famous air acrobatic team, the Red Arrows. Marlene worked as a kitchen assistant in the mess at the airbase, Thomas also did some kitchen work there before his health deteriorated, they had bought a house in Cranwell village that at one time was part of the accommodation for the RAF personnel, he really liked it there.

My son Christopher had completed his naval service and was now a serving police officer on Merseyside. After a couple of run-ins with one or two unsavoury characters, he transferred to the Special Branch, anti-terrorist unit, this meant he had to relocate to Brighton. One particular job that he was on required covert surveillance of a building. He was on the upper floor of the local maternity unit, this gave him good visual access to the building that was being watched, he also had access to a constant stream of coffee and other delights, due to the courtesy of one of the midwives, her name was Samantha. This kindness helped him to relieve the boredom of what would have normally been very tedious operation. Sam had a daughter Hannah, along with Christopher we all met up at Thomas's house for a fun weekend, I think we all went bowling, and then on to one of the clubs on the airbase, we all had a great time and it was also a great opportunity for Sam and Hannah to meet up with their potential future in-laws.

29

Thomas was starting to look and feel much better, we were just about ready to confirm our holiday booking. We were planning a trip to the south of France, many years ago I had a family holiday there with Thomas and Marlene, my ex-shipmate Jimmy Harriet, his wife Bethan, and their two children – a good time was had by all. I asked Thomas if he and Marlene would like to join us, they both agreed that it would be a good idea and something to look forward to. The basic plan was drive to Portsmouth, take the cross-channel ferry to St Malo, then a leisurely drive down south. We rented a gîte in Aigues-Mortes not too far from Montpelier. We had a good time, we booked a boat trip to go and have a look at the bulls, and the wild horses of the Camargue, unfortunately Thomas decided the boat trip didn't appeal to him as it was feeling a bit queasy, he stayed ashore with Marlene as Viv and I went on the trip. When we returned it became obvious that Thomas was unwell, we asked him if he wanted us to take him to a local hospital, naturally he was very apprehensive, the only other alternative was to get him back home to the UK. We terminated the holiday, packed the car, then headed north. We were eventually able to get him to the hospital in Leicester where he had his transplant. When we eventually got him to the hospital he was diagnosed with renal failure, somehow a mistake had been made with his medication so he ended up getting too much potassium, the end result was, irreparable kidney damage, he was now back on dialysis for three days a week. I was very angry and I wanted my pound of flesh. Thomas taught me a lesson in humility that made me feel very humble and proud of him, all he wanted to say to the hospital staff was thank you, for giving me six months without the need for dialysis.

Back at High Canons, work was picking up with plenty to do in the house, as well as working with the film companies. Mrs Noad hosted an annual summer lunch in the Pavilion, for about 30 of their friends and family, due to the numbers a catering company was called in, our brief was to be responsible for the laying of all the tables, meeting and greeting the guests, as well as keeping an eye on the caterers. The afternoon was a brilliant success, during my conversation the boss of the catering company, I was very surprised by how much they were being paid, up until this point I had never felt the need to questioned my salary. A similar occasion arose when Thomas, the eldest son had his 21st birthday party, on the positive side Vivien and I, were invited to the party as guests. Another catering company was hired, and after another conversation I was of the opinion that we were being underpaid. I then made a conscious decision that in the not too distant future, I would be having a discussion with Mr Noad about our pay and conditions. The catering company they hired this time provided the full service, our only input was for advice as to where the band should set up their instruments. David, the younger son, and a couple of his friends were aspiring musicians, they approached me to see if I would ask the band if there be any possibility of them using the PA system, amplifiers and the microphones so they could do a few songs when the band had a break. The boys had their own guitars, the bandleader was very amiable, he was quite happy to let the boys use their speakers and amplifiers. The drummer said that he didn't mind if anybody wanted to use his kit. I relayed this message back to David and his friends, they were all in the library having a practice session – when the band were finished their first set, the bandleader announced that there would be a guest band making a debut performance. All of the guests gathered around the area where the band was set up. David and his three friends where plugging their guitars in, and checking the microphones. David announced that his band needed a drummer and the drummer from the professional band started to make his way forward. David told him no, we want him, he was pointing directly at me. 'Come on Michael, let's see what you've got.' The band's performance went down very well, and I must admit I enjoyed playing again.

There was an old storeroom attached to the cottage that was full of rubbish and junk. Mr Noad gave me his permission to get rid of all the rubbish, and turn it into a second bedroom, this was an ongoing project that I undertook in my own time, when we had friends or family visiting us we were given the use of the apartment for them to stay in, this worked very well. Christopher, Sam and Hannah came for visit one weekend while the family were on holiday, Chris and Sam told us that they were planning to get married, and that their long-term plan was to emigrate to Australia. We were very pleased for them, and we wished them well, but we declined the wedding invitation simply because we wanted to avoid the possibility of any conflict arising with my ex-wife. Christopher agreed with me and accepted my decision, Sam said she would really like us to be there, but she decided that Christopher and I were right and it was probably for the better. As they were living together now a wedding present seemed inappropriate, we offered to make a contribution to the honeymoon fund to the sum of £1000, they were overjoyed – they were planning a honeymoon in Cancun so this donation would be really handy. I got a call from my sister Valerie, she told me that he was coming over to the UK, so we arranged that her and her two daughters, Alison and Laura, should come and stay with us for a week. During the same week that they were with us, we received a call from our friend from St Maarten, Ray, to say he was in the UK and can we have a get-together? We were definitely up for that, we were really looking forward to meeting up with Ray. Vivien and Val went shopping, and I had planned a day out for my two nieces that they would never forget. I was able to get them day visitor passes to the Elstree Film Studios, they had a fabulous time going behind the scenes looking at all the sets and then see some of the models that were used in blockbusters. The following day we all went out together to Thorpe Park, there was one ride in particular that was made famous by the iconic photograph of Princess Diana with her two sons, Princes, William and Harry.

The four of us, Laura, Alison, Ray and myself were now going to try and replicate that photograph. It was against my better judgement, but I was overruled and told to shut up and get in the log. I was in the front, the two girls were behind me, and Ray was in the back – the designers of this ride obviously hadn't taken into consideration what the effect of two grossly overweight gorillas sitting in their log would have on the stability, and gravitational effects of water displacement. The log went down the last slope like a torpedo, instead of gliding across a lake at the bottom, it ploughed through the water like a sperm whale, tons of water cascaded into the log – we couldn't have got any wetter if we were in a shower. I suppose on the upside we were grateful that the lake was shallow otherwise the log would definitely have sunk. Luckily it was a bright sunny day and it didn't take long for us all to drip dry. When the time came for Val and the girls to leave we promised them that our next holiday he would come to visit them in Ireland.

Ray left the following day as he had some business to attend to up north, it was really good to see him.

Vivien's father Tom had been unwell for a long time, we had made a couple of overnight dashes to be at his bedside at the local hospital. He was a tough old guy, after a few days of bed rest he'd be discharged back home to be looked after by his wife Megan. Tom and Megan met each other in the NAAFI during the Second World War. Tom had been serving in North Africa and was home on leave, Megan was serving in the WRAF. Tom's family were quite well off running a garage and the taxi business in the town of Ruthin, Megan's parents were tenant farmers on a farm in Newborough on the Isle of Anglesey. The owner of the farm also owned a holiday cottage quite close to the farmhouse. This gentleman was Maurice Wilks, he designed and built the first Land Rover, he used the farm and the sand dunes as a testing ground for his new design, his basic idea came from the American jeep, but he wanted something that could almost double up as a tractor, and as we know his design for the Land Rover became very, very famous indeed. Vivien's grandmother became good friends with Mr and Mrs Wilks, and also became their de facto housekeeper, looking after their cottage during their absence as well as providing fresh vegetables and dairy produce when they were in residence. Vivien as a young girl spent a lot of time with her grandparents on their farm, She would tag along with her nan to get some on-the-job training from a true professional. Viv became such a fixture with the Wilks's family she was often included with the Wilks's children on the test drives around the sand dunes, she was even taken out on the joy rides around the island on their speedboat.

30

Vivien's sister Susan was due to be married soon and, mainly due to her father's ill-health, she had asked me, 'Would you walk me down the aisle?' I said 'Yes.' She also said that she would like my two nieces to be bridesmaids. Valerie and the girls were overjoyed, plus they were getting another week's holiday in North Wales. All the plans were made with days and dates of travelling confirmed. Tragically Tom, passed away about two weeks before the wedding, Susan and Ian came very close to postponing it, the overriding factor in going ahead with it was that an awful lot of people had made plans and travel arrangements, plus the wedding venue, the church, all of this had taken a considerable amount of time and effort from a lot of people. The wedding went ahead as scheduled, the bride looked beautiful, as did the bridesmaids, for obvious reasons it was a little bit subdued, but on the positive side it was good that all Vivien's family were together. We had planned to spend the rest of the week in North Wales so we could spend a bit more time with Val and the two girls, during that week we got the devastating news that Vivien's uncle passed had away, he was Megan's younger brother Geriant, this was a terrible blow for Megan, losing a husband, and then her youngest brother, she was inconsolable. After a chat with the rest of the family it was agreed that we should take Megan back to High Cannons with us for two weeks. Mr and Mrs Noad were quite amiable to Viv's request to be a little bit more flexible with her working hours.

Mrs Noad even suggested that Vivien should bring Megan with her when she came to work. This worked very well –Vivien had definitely inherited Megan's love of domesticity, and Mrs Noad got two housekeepers for the price of one. On one of our weekends off, the three of us went into the centre of London to take Megan sightseeing. We were very surprised to learn that Megan was quite familiar with London. During the Second World War Megan joined up and she was in the WRAF, she had been posted to the RAF base at Mill Hill where she was working on Barrage Balloons, she had a very traumatic experience, that resulted in her being medically discharged. We have since learnt that a nearby hospital received a direct hit in an air raid and Megan was involved in the rescue attempt, some of the casualties were children.

Megan enjoyed the rest of her stay with us, and one of other daughters had arranged to come and pick her up when she was ready to go back home.

Christopher and Sam's wedding was nearly upon us and it was time for us to make good on the promise of a cash donation to the honeymoon fund. I wrote a very long letter to Chris and Sam, basically saying that things weren't going as well as expected on the job front, things were really hard, same old struggle to make ends meet all the usual platitudes, cash flow crisis, I know you will understand, please find enclosed cheque, and we hope all your plans are going well, I enclosed a cheque for £50. I didn't know Sam that well and I rather hoped that she would see the funny side of the letter. She was not amused, but I did redeem myself by posting a second cheque for £950 the next day. Christopher said, 'I think I saw through your letter, but I was very relieved to receive the next day's post.'

Things were getting very busy at High Cannons, there was a production crew shooting a film that was directed by Mike Leigh, it was called *Topsy Turvy*, featuring Timothy Spall. After the shoot I had a meeting with Mr Noad to discuss our pay and conditions, this was not a very productive meeting.

Mr Noad's opinion was that we had a very nice place to live in.

It was decided that we should look for another job. We started in earnest by sending out our CVs to a couple of the employment agencies that special-ised in domestic service. We had a couple of interviews, with one being very promising, the gentleman that interviewed us called me a couple of days later, regrettably, to tell me we didn't get the job he'd advertised but he asked me if it would be all right for him to send our particulars to a good friend of his in Warwickshire.

I received a call a week later from a Mr Fitzroy Newdigate, he told me that his friend was very impressed, and he was convinced that we were just the couple that he was looking for. He gave me his address and we agreed a day and date for the interview, it had to be on a Sunday as we had to allow a minimum of a six hour round trip, due to the fact that we worked 5 1/2 days a week. The journey to Warwickshire was okay, the directions were to leave the motorway and head for Nuneaton, we were surprised to notice a couple of tourist information road signs guiding tourists to Arbury Hall. We drove through the town of Nuneaton following the signs for Arbury Hall. Stockingford Road was like any other suburban road, tree lined with rows of semi-detached, and detached houses, at the end of the row houses on the left, there were two crenelated towers with a gate, once through the gate there was a small courtyard with another gate, this gate was locked. The person living at the gatehouse had been advised that we were coming so he came out and unlocked the gate he said to me, 'When you return just give a couple of toots on your horn and I will let you out, and good luck with the interview.' The drive through the grounds was amazing, we crossed over the humpbacked bridge and down through a wooded area and came to wall with a big gateway, drove in through the gateway, and into fabulous quadrant. The sight of the building was truly breath-taking, it was like a fairy-tale castle, we were over-whelmed. Vivien even suggested that we drive round the square and back out and not even bother going for the interview, and I must admit the same idea crossed my mind, and it was only due to the fact that the gentleman that let us in at the gate, told me that he had been instructed to telephone Mr Fitzroy Newdigate and tell him that we had arrived. We parked the car, then as we walked through the inner courtyard to the front door we were convinced that this was going to be wasted an afternoon. We spent almost two hours being interviewed by Mr and Mrs Fitzroy Newdigate, the first half-hour would be classed as an interview, then it turned into a very friendly chat. During the conversation it transpired that Mr Fitzroy Newdigate was a keen sailor, and that he had been involved in the ill-fated 1979 Fastnet race, during which 15 sailors lost their lives. That was about the only thing we had in common, but we must have made the right impression, because at the end of the interview they offered us the position of butler and housekeeper. All we had to do was to finalise a starting date, this of course would be subject to how much notice he would have to give at High Cannons. Although we had no contract there, we agreed that we would start in one month, as we left they gave us the security code for the automatic gate that let us leave the estate via another gate, which meant we didn't have to drive back through Nuneaton. On the journey home we reached the unanimous decision that this job was definitely not for us. I felt that we would be hopelessly out of our comfort zone. Vivien agreed wholeheartedly. It was going to be quite late by the time we got home, so I decided I would call Mr Fitzroy Newdigate on the Monday morning and let him know that we would not be accepting his offer of employment. Just before we left for work I called Mr Fitzroy Newdigate and told him that we had a change of heart and that we would not taking up employment with him. I was quite upfront with him and told him we felt that we were out of our depth and that we would be hard pressed to achieve the high standards that were required. He was very surprised and he said he really appreciated my honesty, and before I made a final decision, would I have a word with his wife, I agreed, his wife was not available at the moment, and he said that she would call me within the hour. I called in to see Mr Noad in his office before he left for the city, I told him that we've been offered a new job and asked him, 'How much notice do you require?' He said, 'That is up to you, when do you want to leave pick a day and let me know.' He then left to go to his office in the city. As arranged I was back in the cottage to answer the phone when Mrs Fitzroy Newdigate called – when I explained our misgivings she was adamant that we were more than capable of fitting in, and providing the standard of service that they wanted. My biggest concern was the catering during the shooting season, she reassured me by saying that if it was an issue with the catering she would just send out for a takeaway. This made me feel a little more positive, I promised her I would call her in half an hour after I've had a chat with Vivien. Vivien was aware of the conversation I had with Mr Noad, and after a brief discussion she agreed that we should give the new job a trial. I went back and called Mrs Fitzroy Newdigate and told her that we would come into work for her, and that before the end of the day I would have a leaving date for her. She was very pleased that we had reconsidered.

31

Sometime during the morning Mr Noad made a telephone call to his wife and he must have told her that we would be leaving. Mrs Noad was not very happy, during our lunch break at home, Mr Noad phoned me and asked me if I would mind if he came over to the cottage and had a chat when he finished work. I said, 'Certainly.' When he came in he was amazed at the transformation, he had not been in the cottage since we'd been here, he said, that he might have been a bit hasty with his reaction this morning, and that he would like to talk about the situation. I told him that after the conversation with him this morning, I had called our prospective employer and told them we would be coming to work for them, so how much notice do you require? He said, 'Is this purely about money?' I answered him, 'Yes it is.' His reply was 'I will match whatever salary you have been offered.' 'Thank you for the offer but I've already given my word that I will be coming to work for them.' 'If that is your final word, then I will make up the difference in your pay if you will give me a months' notice.' We agreed that we would leave on December 4th 1999. I called Mr Fitzroy Newdigate and told him that we would be available to start work on Monday, 6th December. He was very pleased and said he was looking forward to working with us. When we renovated the annexe all the materials needed where paid for by Mr Noad, we furnished the cottage at our own expense. The cottage that went with the job at Arbury Hall was a new build, and it came completely furnished, all we needed were our toothbrushes. Mr Noad agreed buy all of the furnishings. Over the next couple of weeks we started to pack all our personal belongings, when it looked like we were going to have a full car we decided it might be practical to drive up to Warwickshire a couple of days before and empty it. We also had bought a small car for Vivien to learn to drive in. I called Mr Fitzroy Newdigate, he said it would be fine and he would make sure that the keys for dairy cottage would be left at the gatehouse.

David, Mr and Mrs Noad's son offered to help us out with the move by volunteering to drive one of the cars. He drove our car with Viv as his passenger, I followed up behind in Viv's car.

David was very impressed when he saw Arbury Hall. We unloaded the contents of both cars into the cottage and we left Viv's car there, then we drove back to Hertfordshire. The date we had chosen to leave happened to be my birthday, as a birthday treat, and a farewell gesture, Mr and Mrs Noad, Thomas and David, invited Vivien and I out to their favourite restaurant in a little town of Bushey for dinner, we were both quite touched by this gesture.

It was really nice to be leaving on such good terms. While we were in the restaurant, there was a bit of interest in a group that had just arrived, as the group passed our table I saw a very familiar face. I remarked, 'Was that who I think it is?' 'Yes,' replied Mrs Noad, 'he comes here quite often.' Vivien was sitting opposite me so she had her back to the group as they passed, she didn't see him. When she asked Mrs Noad, 'Who is it?' she replied, 'It's Sir Cliff Richard.' Vivien insisted that we change places so she could see, unfortunately their party was in a secluded alcove so wasn't much to see. Mr and Mrs Noad had given me a birthday card at the restaurant, much to everybody's amazement, Vivien picked the birthday card up, left the table and went over and introduced herself to Sir Cliff Richard, and politely asked him, 'Would you mind signing my husband's birthday card please?'. 'Certainly,' he replied, 'how could I refuse such a gracious request?' He signed the card, and as he passed it back to her he took her hand, and like the true gentleman that he is, kissed the back of it. Vivien was ecstatic, and I've got a card with a personalised birthday greeting from Sir Cliff Richard. The rest of the evening was a fabulous success we had a great time with the family, and there was a slight hint of sadness from all concerned when it came time to say goodnight. The whole family turned out the next day to say farewell, and wished us good luck with our new venture.

32

Arbury Hall, is a 16th-century Elizabethan manor house that was built on the site of an Augustine monastery that, at the time of the dissolution of the monasteries in 1536, had been razed – most of the materials from the demolition were used by Sir Edmund Anderson to build Arbury Hall. In 1582 he was appointed chief justice of the Common Pleas at the court of Elizabeth I. It was very inconvenient for him to travel from Arbury to London so, in 1586, by mutual agreement he exchanged it for Harefield Place Middlesex, this was the property of John Newdigate. His son, also named John, married Anne Fitton, whose sister Mary was maid of honour to Queen Elizabeth I, reputedly a very beautiful lady but, with questionable morality – rumour also has it he may have been a shady character of Shakespeare's poems. The current owners of the Arbury estate were Francis Humphrey Fitzroy Newdigate, 3rd Viscount Daventry, and his wife, Lady Rosemary. Sir Humphrey Fitzroy Newdigate was ADC to Lord Louis Mountbatten, the Viceroy of India 1946–1948, he was also an accomplished cricketer playing for both Northamptonshire and Warwickshire, he was Lord-Lieutenant of Warwickshire from 1990 to 1997.

He became the 3rd Viscount Daventry in 1986. It was very interesting when we were shown round the hall to see pictures of Lady Daventry as a young girl playing with the future Queen Elizabeth II, these were now the exalted circles that we now found ourselves up to our necks in, no pressure there then. They had three children, James, Hugh and their sister Joanna. Mr and Mrs James Fitzroy Newdigate and their two children, Humphrey, and Hester. Humphrey was four years of age, his sister Hester was nearly three years old, they employed a full-time nanny, two au pairs, and three part-time cleaners. The cleaning ladies were mainly responsible for the corporate side of the hall that on occasion was open to the general public. Due to the deteriorating health of Lord Daventry, his eldest son and family had moved back to live at the hall in a wing that had been very tastefully renovated to meet the needs of a growing family. Our remit was to look after the property and the needs of the family. During the shooting season there were a number of shooting parties; the normal process for a weekend shoot involved getting the guest rooms ready, procuring, preparing, cooking and serving the food for the family and their guests. Some of the guests would arrive on Friday, late afternoon, there would be dinner in the family wing of the hall, on Saturday morning there would be a full English breakfast. There would be additional guests arriving, after the shoot there would be an afternoon tea, we would prepare sandwiches and freshly made scones, at about 8 pm a formal dinner would be held in the main dining room. On Sunday morning there would be another full English breakfast, and finally lunch, a typical Sunday roast in the dining room. We would start work at 7 am on Friday till about midnight; Saturday morning start at 6.30 am till about 1am; then Sunday start at 7.30 am to 4 pm. On a Tuesday we would have a meeting with Mrs Fitzroy Newdigate to discuss the plan for the weekend, she would have her list of guest numbers, she would allocate the various guest rooms that were to be used, and by whom, we would then go through menus for all the meals through the weekend. I didn't see any takeaway menus. We didn't have the benefit of any trial run, we were thrown in the deep end with a shooting party for the first weekend we were there. It would take me about two hours to dress the dining room, the dining table could seat 6 or 36. I needed two men for fitting or removing the additional leaves so the size of the table could be tailored suit the amount of diners. When the table was fully dressed it was spectacular, there was probably enough silverware and crystal there to settle the national debt of many of the Third World countries. It took a few days to familiarise ourselves with the layout of the many rooms that we had to access for security reasons, every door and window was protected by intruder alarms, when the family were not in residence all doors and windows had to be checked daily. The family kept a house in London, so for whatever the reason they were in the city they always had somewhere to stay. As I was preparing the car for them Mrs Fitzroy said to me, 'Well Michael this is our moment of truth, it will be interesting to see if that the family silver is still here when we return.' I replied, 'The family silver will be quite safe Ma'am as I can't remember exactly where the strong room is located.'

As we were getting more familiar with our surroundings and after the success of the first shoot we started to relax a little more, only to have the rug well and truly pulled from under our feet. Upon their return from London, Mrs Fitzroy Newdigate, informed me that they would be having a millennium celebration party with their family and friends; we would be catering for about 30 guests, this was going to be a big ask. I knew that we would need extra help. I called my brother Thomas see how he was and, if it was on, 'How do you and Marlene fancy a couple of days as my galley slaves?' He said, that he was 'fit and well and that would be no problem.' I spoke to Mr Fitzroy, and he was quite happy to hire the both of them for the three-day holiday, I called Thomas to confirm the arrangement and he said, 'Looking forward to it, see you on Thursday.' Thomas and Marlene duly arrived, it was hard work for him but he'd done well and when he was called in and presented to the guests in the dining room he was given a standing ovation. The only downside was when we finally realised that Marlene had a major drink problem. Marlene had a sister that lived in Nuneaton, so to prevent any further awkwardness Thomas drove her to a sister's house and told her he would pick her up when he finished at Arbury. It is impossible to even try to comprehend the stress, and levels of despair, depression, and desperation that Marlene has to deal with on a daily basis due to Thomas's ill-health, so with the benefit of hindsight, it's quite easy to see how Marlene acquired such a dependency on alcohol.

The millennium celebrations were a storming success, a good time was had by one and all. We had one more shoot to prepare for in January, having had the benefit of a professional chef in the kitchen, that took some of the pressure off me. It allowed me a little more latitude in the saloon with pre-dinner drinks and hors d'oeuvres. So, for the Saturday night dinner Mrs Fitzroy Newdigate was quite happy to employ a professional chef. Unfortunately this did not guarantee success, on one occasion the main course was a duck breast, which was inedible, the dessert, was a poached pear with a toffee sauce, the pears were rock hard and couldn't be served, the kitchen has an oil fired Aga, and an electric range cooker, the chef was desperately trying to soften the pears, she was distracted, she forgot about the pan of toffee sauce that was on the Aga – to say it boiled over would be an understatement, it erupted like a mini volcano and covered the top of the Aga in toffee sauce. Fortunately she was using the electric range cooker for the pears. 'Don't worry,' she said, 'I will be able to salvage some and if we haven't got enough sauce, I can serve the rest with ice cream.' There was a sudden swoosh, and the entire top of the Aga burst into flame. I don't know how, but I managed to get the pan of the top of the Aga and into the sink, then I tried to smother the flames with a fire blanket. I also needed a fire extinguisher, at this moment in time the kitchen looked like a war zone full of smoke and steam – that set the fire alarm off. I ran into the dining room and a quick word with Mr Fitzroy Newdigate. I told him 'everything was under control no cause for concern.' I then had to dash along the corridor to the control panel to cancel the alarm call, I was about two seconds too late the fire crew had just been dispatched. I called the gatekeeper and told him to expect a couple of fire engines, and that he should tell the fire team that everything was under control. When the fire chief arrived at the gate told the gatekeeper that he had to come down to the hall and check for himself, and that he was satisfied that the fire had been dealt with. All of the guests were quite impressed with the sight of a dozen or so of strapping firefighters, it was a small compensation for the ruined dinner. The only upside was, after a meeting with the fire chief he decided we needed a salvage plan just in case there was a serious fire, a lot of the contents were irreplaceable and probably priceless. Once the shooting season had finished we had an appraisal meeting and we were pleased with the outcome, the only mishaps, fortunately were not of our doing, we were given a couple of days off so we went and spent a long weekend in Lincoln with Thomas and Marlene.

When we returned to work, we were greeted with the news that the nanny had left. I can recall Humphrey's first day at preschool, I think it was at Market Bosworth, he looked ever so grown-up in his first school uniform.

The new nanny duly arrived, her name was Julie, she was from Kegworth, just outside Nottingham. Julie had some issues at home, I got the impression this was just a stopgap job for her. It was a very sad time for the family, tragically Lord Daventry passed away on the 15th February, and while the family was still in shock, his son Hugh, Mr Fitzroy Newdigate's younger brother passed away during the first week of May during a business trip to Rangoon. That meant Mr Fitzroy Newdigate inherited the title and became the 4th Viscount Daventry, we were now employed by a titled family. The family always had their annual summer holiday in Cornwall, they also took the nanny and the au pair with them, that left us with two weeks of semi-freedom, which allowed us to completely overhaul both the family kitchen, and the corporate kitchen. I would have to call in an engineer to service the burners on the Aga, everything else, Vivien and I took care of. This became an annual event, it was always very nice compliment, to hear Lady Daventry say that no matter where she went on holiday, she always looked forward to coming back home to her own personal executive housekeeper, and her pristine kitchen. We had our first week's holiday so we went to Amsterdam, the date of the holiday coincided with a three-day Tall Ships Regatta, it was a fabulous holiday, we took the ferry from Dover to Calais, then had a leisurely drive across to Amsterdam. We had booked into the Intercontinental Amstel Hotel, this was canal side, right in the city centre it was a perfect location for a canal cruise that included a full tour of all the docks where tall ships were berthed.

We had done all the touristy things, with the odd one or two exceptions, We didn't do the wacky baccy cafes, but we did have a look at some of the more dubious establishments offering slightly more than a teacake laced with hash, and no we didn't partake. There was a party-like atmosphere in every bar we went into, with our booze-addled brains we sort of staggered back to where we thought the hotel was. Vivien was desperate for the little girls room, we went into one particular establishment, Vivien went off in search of the loo, I went to the bar to order a drink. The lighting was very subdued, the atmosphere was very oppressive, with very heavy strange background music thumping, a guy appears next to me and asked, 'Are you on holiday?' I said, 'No I'm just here for the tall ships.' He replied, 'Oh do you like sailors then?' Just about now my eyes were getting accustomed to the light, as I looked around the bar I could just about make out that the bar was full of men all appearing to be quite friendly to each other, then the penny dropped, We were in a gay bar, I was very relieved when Vivien appeared, we left without ordering drinks.

We laughed about it all the way back to the hotel, the next day Viv woke up with the hangover from hell, she was feeling dreadful, we had one more day to stay but she pleaded with me to get in the car and let's head for home. We checked out, retrieved the car from the car park and set off, after only ten minutes we had to stop, Vivien was very ill, and the thought of a very long drive to Calais filled her with trepidation. We decided to head for the Hook of Holland, a much shorter drive and then the ferry to Harwich, this would have given her another four to five hours on the horizontal. The only downside to this detour was that our return ticket for the Calais to Dover ferry was useless, so I had to buy a very expensive one-way ticket back to the UK. The drive back to Arbury was very uneventful, she slept most of the way home, and then she went straight to bed, there is a lesson in there somewhere.

Julie the nanny was still having problems with her personal life so she had to leave. Her daughter Emma, became the new nanny. In my opinion she was totally unsuitable, she had no concept of professional childcare, she was just a babysitter that slept over.

When Hester started preschool I began to spend more time doing the school runs with both of the children. Lady Daventry had taken a position on the board of Laura Ashley, and Lord Daventry was involved with one of the large insurance companies in the city, that meant that both of them would have to spend a little more time away from home. Due to the high standards that were required for the catering of the shooting parties, and the less formal dinner parties for the family and friends, both Vivien and I enrolled at the local college for evening classes to improve, and perfect our cooking abilities, this we both enjoyed, and it also gave us more confidence in the kitchens.

Outside of the shooting season the level of activity concerning entertaining and dinner parties was greatly reduced, so we had plenty of opportunities to put our newly acquired skills to the test – also due to the fact that Lady Daventry was expecting their third child, so the frequency of dinner parties had been greatly reduced. On Tuesday March 8th 2001 Lady Daventry gave birth to her second daughter Sofia Hebe. She was absolutely adorable it was definitely love at first sight. The family were planning a winter skiing holiday, I can recall a conversation that I had with Lady Daventry. I was expressing my concern over what I considered to be the unsuitability of the current nanny to look after Hebe properly, 'Oh! There's no cause for concern there Michael, Hebe can stay here with you and Vivien in your cottage.' Well that was a done deal then, we brought her cot over to the cottage and the bonding process continued. Upon their return from the skiing holiday, as a thank you gesture for our impromptu nannying services, we were given some additional time off. We put this to good use by renting an apartment on the Costa Brava.

The couple who owned the villa where the apartment was that we rented were expat Brits that had retired to the Spanish sun. We got on very well with them, and as per normal I ended up being their handyman for a few days. They even offered us the opportunity to manage their business for them. Once again we had to think of all the benefits of being back in the UK, against the prospects of a more laid-back lifestyle living in the sun. We declined their offer. Their next-door neighbours had allowed them to use one of their outbuildings for storage, that included the use of a large freezer. One day after a busy visit to the supermarket she had a few items that needed to go into the neighbour's freezer. The neighbour had two dogs, these were semi-guard dogs that had free access to the property, the procedure before she entered the property was to shout to the owner to let them know she was at the gate. The neighbour told her that the dogs were locked up and it was safe to come on in, not sure how it happened, but one of the dogs was on the loose and it attacked her, the injuries were so severe she ended up having one of her arms amputated. Shortly after that they both came back to the UK – it was obviously an horrendous accident, but it was obvious to us that we had made the right decision. I had been experiencing some difficulties in walking, it transpired that I had a bunion on my left foot that required attention, my GP advised me that there was a long waiting list for this procedure. Lord Daventry sent me to a private specialist, the procedure was done and I was told that I must get plenty of rest and no driving, this six-week layup was just the catalyst that we needed to push Vivien into making a supreme effort to take up driving lessons again. To be told that I wouldn't be able to wear a shoe for the next six weeks was mildly amusing, but I must admit it was very uncomfortable, and I did have to spend an awful lot of time sitting with my feet up. On one particular day the TV was on in the background, and suddenly one scene grabbed my attention, at first it appeared that I was watching the replay of a disaster blockbuster, then it dawned on me that this was a live news broadcast, it was surreal to actually watch one building in flames, then to see an aircraft crash into the second building – this was 911 as it happened. Lady Daventry had taken the decision to bring in some temporary help until I was literally back on my feet. I think it was about this time that Emma, the nanny, decided it was time to leave, no surprise there then. The new nanny duly arrived, her name was Debbie, she was from Howden in east Yorkshire, she looked and acted, just like a professional nanny.

33

The next shooting season came and ended without any major hiccups, things were getting back to normal, we would spend our time off between Lincoln, and North Wales. If the family were not in residence during a weekend, because of the security implications, naturally we had to stay on the property, if any of our family or friends wanted to come and visit us we would always try to arrange their visit so it coincided with a time that the family were not at home. On one such planned visit Vivien's brother Kevin, his wife Christine, and their daughter Charlotte arranged to come for a weekend visit – the family, their nanny, and all their luggage had to be at Birmingham airport for about 5:30 am on Saturday morning. We had to take two cars, my brother-in-law Kevin offered his services, I took Lady Daventry, the children, and the nanny in the people carrier. Lord Daventry and the luggage followed in his car, Kevin drove his car back, during the drive to the airport. Kevin and Lord Daventry were having a conversation about fishing and Lord Daventry gave Kevin permission to fish in any of the lakes on the estate. Kevin was ecstatic as he was a keen fisherman. On his next visit he made sure he brought his fishing gear with him, he thought he had died and gone to heaven. On one occasion he was approached by the gamekeeper and quite rightly told the gamekeeper that Lord Daventry had personally given him his permission to fish the lakes, the gamekeeper replied, 'Sorry to bother you sir.' The irony of the situation did not go unnoticed – Kevin, as a youngster was not averse to a little salmon and trout poaching to supplement his meagre pocket money.

We had some time so for our next holiday we decided to go down to Cornwall. We rented a cottage not far from Padstow, there was now a bridge over the River Camel not far from Wadebridge. It was just as well we left when we did as it was a fixed bridge and we would not have been able to sail underneath it. Obviously we went down to Charlestown, nothing had changed there it was still a quaint Victorian harbour, we continued playing tourists thoroughly enjoying our trip down memory lane. In the village of St Minver, there was a small church St Enodoc – there was a memorial there that caught my attention, it made reference to a recent shipwreck just outside Padstow, the ship was called the *Maria Asumpta*, regrettably three people lost their lives.

The *Maria Asumpta* was the re-registered name of the sailing vessel, *The Inca*, this vessel was the sister ship of *The Marques*, they both worked out of Charlestown. When we got back home I done a little more research on both of the ships, *The Marques*, had been re-rigged to resemble the HMS *Beagle*, for a BBC television series on Charles Darwin. This was the same vessel that had been lost in the Tall Ships Race. I was intrigued when I read that in 1828 during a prolonged cartographic survey, that the Master of the *Beagle*, Capt. Pringle Stokes, committed suicide by shooting himself. Robert Fitzroy was a young first lieutenant, so he assumed command, the ship completed the survey and returned to the UK. He was promoted to captain and was commissioned to complete an additional survey of the Pacific Ocean. Due to the solitude of a four or five-year voyage one of Capt. Fitzroy's relatives paid for the services of gentleman scientist to accompany him on this long and tedious voyage, the scientist was Charles Darwin, they became great friends. Capt. Fitzroy was instrumental in setting up the weather forecasting system as we know it today, he also invented the first barometer, he also set up a storm warning system that operates in every harbour in the UK. He retired as an Admiral. Then in 2002 the Admiralty renamed the shipping area from, Finisterre to Fitzroy, in memory of his achievement in the field of weather forecasting.

I had a conversation with Lord Daventry and I asked him was there any family connection to Admiral Fitzroy? He replied, 'Yes Michael he was my great, great, great, grandfather,' and he showed me the original barometer, along with his notes and drawings.

We were living very comfortably with very little in the way of outgoings, so we decided that we should try to buy a house for our retirement. Due to Thomas's fragile state of health we were of the opinion that we should be quite close to where he lived.

We went along to the local building society in Coventry and found that we were prime candidates for a mortgage. Because of the distance travelling from Arbury to Cranwell, Thomas and Marlene agreed to go house hunting for us, and to make a shortlist of any of the properties that they thought would suit us. Over a month we must of visited at least half a dozen properties, the one that we all thought was ideal was an ex-railway signal man's house, and it was perfect – that was until the 3.15 steel train on its way to Skegness thundered past, it bore a strange resemblance to Hurricane Louis.

The estate agent said they had another property in the village of Billinghay, that was in need of some work, it was about 25 minutes away from Crawnwell. We agreed to go and have a look, the estate agent was on a tight schedule so she gave us the keys and asked us to drop them off at the office in Sleaford after we had viewed the property. We pulled up outside the house, it had curb appeal. But that was where it ended. It was double-fronted with the window on the right hand side of the door being twice the size of the one on the left hand side of the door, this looked like had been a shop window. This house had been professionally gutted by a very disgruntled previous owner, due to the property being repossessed, every electrical outlet and switch had been cut off so close to the wall that it would be impossible to reconnect them, the whole house needed rewiring, the kitchen consisted of about nine inches of lead pipe that came up through the floor under the window, every other tile on the walls had been hit with a ball hammer, the bathroom was devoid of any fittings, with just a hole in the floor where the WC should be connected. Vivien, Thomas, and Marlene were all of the same opinion that the house was a wreck, I had to agree with them, but I could see the potential. Viv was horrified. 'Do you really think that you could renovate this house?' she asked. 'All it's going to take is time and money,' was my reply. We went back to the estate agent, put an offer in, and it was accepted. Upon our return to Arbury we went along to the building society, did the deal, now the house was ours. I made a wish list and started in earnest to acquire everything that I was going to need for the renovation. Lord Daventry was very helpful, he gave me the use of one of the old sheds that I could use for storing items that I bought – this included boxes of electrical fittings, coils of cable, 65 boxes of laminate flooring, and a complete second-hand kitchen. Most of these items were all bought at the local auction house, he also let me use the estate Land Rover and trailer. Our first priority was an electrician, fortunately my newest brother-in-law, Ian, Susan's husband, was an electrician, he worked for himself. All four of us decided that during our next annual holiday, we would move into the house for two weeks and begin the renovation. On one of our visits we were very surprised to find out that we also owned the driveway at the side of the house that led to a fair-sized plot of land. Thomas was able to find, and get delivered to the site, a small touring caravan that we were able to connect to the water supply; we were also able to fit a WC in the upstairs bathroom of the house, all was well, we had a usable bathroom, as well as running water. There was also a working fireplace, what more could you ask for? We sorted out a date for our two-week holiday, and agreed to meet Ian and Susan just outside Grantham, then we drove to Billinghay to start the marathon. There was a fish and chip shop in the village, and a Chinese takeaway a couple miles down the road in Tattershall. We didn't go hungry as Thomas had provided his own take on the meals on wheels service. We were more than satisfied with the rate of progress and by the time it came to leave, we had electricity, hot and cold water in the kitchen, and a working toilet in the bathroom. One of the neighbours made a comment about the legal issues concerning the occupation of the caravan and that I should have the position clarified by the local council, as we were going to the council for the advice Thomas was of the opinion that if council were okay with it, we could he put at new chalet unit on the plot, and he would happily live in it. I met with the council official and told him that my brother was a disabled ex-serviceman and would the council have any objections if I put a new mobile home on the plot for my brother to live in. He couldn't think of any objections, but he recommended that we submit a planning application. I said 'Thank you for your advice.' He asked me about access to the plot and how big it was, when I told him he said, 'Why don't you submit a planning application to build him a new bungalow?' I said, 'Thank you very much I will take it under advisement.'

34

Both Vivien and Thomas were taken aback at the suggestion of a new build, we said we would explore all possibilities the next time we return so we should have a battle plan.

We decided that we would have another mini-break in Amsterdam, but this time we were able to fulfil Megan's lifelong dream, she had always wanted to see the Dutch tulip fields, again we went by car via the cross-channel ferry booked into a really nice hotel at Schiphol airport. We took her to the beautiful Keukenhof Gardens, she really enjoyed the sights and the smells of all the flowers. When we were leaving I went to check out at reception and I was horrified to see an astronomical charge for the mini-bar in Megan's room, I made an excuse and went back to the room to find that Megan had emptied the contents of the mini-bar into her bag. She was not happy when I asked her to put it all back, she was convinced it was all complementary. I went back down to reception and explained that my mother-in-law emptied the fridge to clean it and it was now restocked, we still laugh at that now.

We were glad to get back to Arbury. It was late August and the family were all away, because of the bank holiday the Hall and Gardens had been open to the public. When the last tour had finished the guide, and the administrator would come and advise me that the Hall was ready to be secured. It was my job to go and check every room that the public had access to, all of the windows had to be shuttered and barred, all internal doors are to be closed so I could test the alarm system, only when everything was sealed could the alarm system be set.

There was a repeater panel in our bungalow, at about 2.30 am the alarm was activated. I have to call the alarm company, give the necessary password and go and check as to why the alarm was triggered, the occasional false alarm was not unusual. Normally, it could be one of the doors along the cloisters. I checked my panel in the cottage, I was surprised to see that the alarm had been activated on the family wing in the library, this was worrying. I done a quick check around the outside ground floor windows, all was okay. Time to go inside, armed

with my trusty baseball bat. I half expected that someone had been on one of the tours and hidden themselves away waiting till all was quiet. I checked every room on the family wing, listening very carefully outside the door to the library, no sounds came from within. I opened the door, turned the lights on, only to be confronted by a bat – it was impossible to catch it, and I would not be able to reset the alarm. The normal procedure would be to call the alarm company again and advise them that the problem had been solved, they would give me a code that I could enter and that would allow me to reset the alarm. This was not going to happen because every time the bat moved it would set the alarm off. I told the operator that I had tried to catch the bat, he told me to be 'very careful as it is probably on the endangered species list.' I replied, 'If gets me out of bed at three o'clock in the morning again, it will be on the extinct list.'

Both Humphrey and Hester were attending the same school at Twycross, for whatever reasons there were times when I would have to go and collect them. One day in particular while I was waiting outside with all the other yummy mummies, one of the teachers approached me. 'Are you Michael?' she asked. 'Yes,' I replied. 'What exactly is it that you do? 'I look after the family, why do you ask?' 'Humphrey insists on telling everybody that you are a pirate.' 'He's not wrong, I did sail a square-rigged sailing ship around the Caribbean.' Occasionally the estate would host lavish corporate events, these were put on by professional companies, they would erect beautiful pavilions with huge mobile kitchens that were capable of producing stunning looking banquets, again all that we had to do was hover in the background and liaise with the event management team. On one occasion it was a food supply companies national awards, there was a banquet for about 300 guests, various celebrities making presentations, plus entertainment. In another pavilion, there was an all-night buffet with a live band, and the grand finale was a fabulous fireworks display incorporating dancing water. Both Vivien and I were invited as guests, we were introduced to some of the celebrities, who included, Frankie

Dettori, Sanjeev Bhaskar, Meera Syal – these were really nice pleasant people. We were also introduced to Gordon Ramsay, his reputation describes him perfectly.

Lady Daventry is a close personal friend of the actress Elizabeth Hurley, both, Lord and Lady Daventry were invited to their wedding celebrations in India. Miss Hurley was a frequent guest at Arbury, she was a beautiful person inside and out, I can remember one occasion when one of her priceless gowns needed pressing. Vivien was very apprehensive of handling the gown. Vivien took it back to her room and knocked on the door. Miss Hurley called her and asked her to bring the dress in. Vivien entered the room and was surprised to see Miss Hurley sitting at the dressing table waiting for her dress, now that was one errand that I wished I had undertaken, she was very complimentary about Vivien's ironing skills. We were getting really comfortable with the way we were fitting in with the family, there was a closeness that transcends the normal employer–employee relationship, this was probably due to how well we got on with the children. And the relationship with Hebe was unique, again this would be due to the fact that she was born while we were there so we were part of her growing up. The usual procedure was that the ten o'clock we have a tea break in the corporate kitchen, when Hebe was at home she would always come and join us for tea and biscuits. She would insist on sitting on my lap and she would dunk her biscuits in my tea. If I was not there she would tag along with Vivien and go through the motions of being an apprentice housekeeper.

Things were getting a bit complicated at home for Thomas due to Marlene's alcohol dependency, which culminated in her being hospitalised on a couple of occasions. Thomas felt that the only option left open to him was for him to move out. He was living in a mobile home on a site just outside Sleaford, he would still pop round to see if she was okay and take her shopping, and to the local bingo hall twice a week. Both Viv and I would continue to use our time off to carry on with the renovations. It was starting to look good. Before we knew it another shooting season was upon us, so we steeled ourselves and now we were better skilled and more confident to step into the breach. The season went well, but I must admit I found it really hard work, the long hours, and being on your feet all day. I found it quite draining. I had a bit of a psoriasis problem on my feet, this did not help. At the end of the season I had a meeting with Lord Daventry and I told him that it was highly unlikely that I would be able to continue working at this level due to my health concerns, he was very sympathetic and he understood my concerns. We agreed that I would give him at least six months' notice, that would give him plenty of time to find a replacement couple, he also asked me would I mind

vetting the applications and sorting out a shortlist of candidates for our replacements once the position had been advertised. During this period Vivien had taken, and failed two driving tests, but she still had a very positive attitude and was convinced that with a little more practise the next one would be the one. On our next visit to Billinghay I had arranged to meet with an architect to discuss the site and the planning application. The meeting was very productive, it was decided that it would be a self-build project using a timber frame construction system, and we submitted a planning application. When planning permission was granted we did some research and we found a company in Hereford that fitted the bill. We went along to the factory sorting out the package that we needed, paid the deposit and came away feeling very pleased with ourselves. That was short-lived, I received a notification from the council to say that the planning permission was issued in error and that I needed to resubmit. This I did, and the planning permission was refused. I had to seek legal advice, this did not come cheap. I amended the planning application and resubmitted it, this again was refused, but I was advised to complain to the planning ombudsman, all of this was taking time. Back at Arbury the couple that were due to replace us had been chosen, we agreed that we would leave at the end of July. Kevin and Chris came for their final visit that included a day's fishing for him. The following day we had rented a van and Kevin and I were going to take the last load of our belongings to Billinghay, also on this day Chris had gone with Vivien to Nuneaton for Vivien's driving test, this time she passed, we were all very pleased and proud of her, and as it was her birthday in July as well, so I bought her a car.

A couple of days before we were due to leave all of the staff gathered together in the dining room for a farewell afternoon tea; along with their good wishes we also received some very nice farewell gifts, it was very touching.

Lord and Lady Daventry took us both out for a farewell dinner to a really nice restaurant. Lady Daventry told us that both Hester and Hebe were really upset at the prospect of Vivien and I leaving, but even more surprising, was Humphrey's reaction. He had told his mother, 'I will really miss the conversations we had mainly during the school runs.' Lady Daventry told him, 'Not to worry we will get a another driver to take you to school.' Humphrey said to his mother, 'Where are you going to find another pirate?' This amused all of us. On the day we left all of the children were at school so there was nobody there to actually see us off. My final act was to go up on to the roof and remove the house standard from the flagpole and I replaced it with a rather large Skull and Crossbones, that Humphrey refused steadfastly to have it taken down. We have since learnt that Humphrey was very impressed with my leaving gift to him.

35

We had planned a holiday to Spain with Avril and Dennis – this went well but I was still feeling under the weather so I didn't really enjoy it and I was glad to get back home. All the work on the house of being completed and it had been done to a very high standard and we were very pleased with the outcome.

Christopher, Sam and Hannah came for a visit and they told us they were emigrating to Australia and that as soon as they were settled he must come out to visit them, we thought that was a brilliant idea. We made a few enquiries that included arranging dialysis for Thomas, this was all done we went ahead and booked the flights. Tibbles, Vivien's little cat lost the last of its nine lives, we had this cat just over 22 years. Vivien was very sad when the vet had to end its suffering. We took it home and buried it in the plot, after about a month she acquired a new cat, Charlotte, we called her Charlie for short. Vivien found a job as a care assistant at a privately run care home just outside Sleaford, and she was thoroughly enjoying her newfound independence. We had to register with a new GP after an initial check-up with the nurse, she suggested that I see the doctor. The doctor I saw was Dr Hinchcliffe, after a short examination he made an appointment for me at the rapid response cardiac unit at the Lincoln Gen Hospital, the subsequent tests confirmed I had a major heart problem. I was then referred to the cardiac unit at Glenfield Hospital just outside Leicester. I was diagnosed as needing a replacement aortic valve and a triple bypass, oops! That crept up on me. The procedure was planned for May, the hospital provided accommodation at a nominal rent for immediate family. Avril stayed with Viv at the apartment, there were complications, the procedure should have taken five hours, it ended up taking just over eight hours. I was transferred to the ITU when Viv and Avril were allowed to come and see me. Vivien was very distressed she said, 'You look like a corpse.' They both went back to the apartment, then things took a turn for the worse. I had to be taken back into the theatre when it became apparent that I was in trouble, the nurse called Vivien and told her to come back to the ITU. It was just after midnight, the nurse then told Vivien and Avril to prepare themselves for the worst. This was due to me developing metabolic acidosis. It took the team a few hours to stabilise me, I was then returned back to the ITU and I woke up two days later. Professor Galinanes who led the team, had told Vivien that it was touch and go as to whether I was going to survive, and he couldn't understand how it was that I had never suffered a heart attack. After I was transferred back onto the ward I had vague memories of people shouting and cheering as I hovered on the brink, I thought I was hallucinating, the following day the guy in the next bed, said to me, 'You're a Scouser how could you possibly sleep through such an important football match?' apparently, it was one of Liverpool's finest European Cup wins.

Once I was off the endangered species list, both Vivien and Avril vacated the apartment, Dennis came and collected Avril. I will always be eternally grateful to Avril for being there for Viv during that very harrowing time.

During my recuperation on the ward, Kevin, Christine and Charlotte made the trip up from North Wales to come and visit me, they then spent a full day with Vivien at Lincoln, and they promised to come back as soon as I was well enough to receive visitors.

Viv went back home to Billinghay, it was about a 130 mile round trip for her to visit me so she shared the driving with Thomas. This only involved one visit – Viv was horrified. Thomas was as blind as a bat and she refused to get in a car with him again. Unfortunately, Viv was only licensed to drive an automatic, so she didn't enjoy the drive back home. Viv was able to sort out a visiting rota between people from Arbury, her brother Kevin, and her sister Avril, so I didn't go short of visitors. I was discharged with a list of to-dos, and not-to-dos; one of the not to dos, was no driving for at least six weeks. We were really pleased that Viv had passed her driving test.

We also received some brilliant news from Australia, Christopher had telephoned to inform was that Sam had given birth to their first son, they called him Corey, we were all overjoyed.

Thomas had to go into hospital at Lincoln. There was a bus stop outside the newsagents in the village. I asked the guy in the shop about the bus timetable for Lincoln, he said he was going to Lincoln in an hour and that he would give me a lift. 'Thank you,' I said when he dropped me off at the hospital, that was quite painless and Thomas was really glad to see me. 'How did you get here?' he asked. I told him, he then said, 'How are you getting home?' 'I'll get the bus,' I said. 'You'll be lucky,' was his reply. He wasn't kidding, three different bus, and one train, journey later, I arrived home to find one very irate wife that was only minutes away from calling the police to report a missing person. I was told in no uncertain terms that I was banned from leaving the house for any reason whatsoever until I acquired a mobile phone. I still don't own one.

My recuperation was nothing short of spectacular, so much so that I was thrown off the rehabilitation course that I was on, because most of the other participants were basket cases, and they all thought they were ill. My GP, Dr Hinchcliffe, was so impressed with my rate of recovery that he asked me would I mind meeting with one of his patients to try and reassure him that the surgery he was awaiting was quite safe. As soon as I was able to drive again, my first job was to take Thomas to the optician for an eye test. Wow! did he need glasses. Marlene's health took a turn for the worse, we got a call to inform us that she had been admitted to hospital again, she was in hospital in Grantham. This was far too frequent, she was really unwell.

Kevin, Christine and Charlotte, true to their word, came over to Lincoln to stay for a weekend, they arrived late Friday afternoon, we got them settled and comfortable. The food we prepared went down very well after the girls had cleared up Kevin and I just sat around the dining table putting the world to rights and talking endless drivel, this was only interrupted by the occasional getting up to replenish the glasses. I had a nice Remy Martin in the drinks cabinet that I had been saving for a special occasion, this seemed special enough. Kevin expressed an opinion that he was not very fond of brandy so I suggested that he tried it in a French coffee. He was very impressed and was converted immediately to the finer points of a good cognac. Needless to say we sat there for hours just enjoying the moment.

The following day we had planned a trip into Lincoln for some Christmas shopping, Kevin was feeling a little bit fragile, complaining that he had a hangover from hell. 'I have never been this sick before he said you must've slipped me a Mickey Finn.' The shopping was a very subdued affair so we decided to head back to Billinghay and chill out for the rest of the evening. Plans were made to go to Skegness on the Sunday morning to continue the shopping spree, this was going well, Viv popped into a shop to buy a serving dish, we all carried on up the street. Kev, Chris and Charlotte went into another shop. I decided to stay outside the doorway to wait for Viv. I saw her coming up the street towards me as she got about ten feet away from me she tripped and her forward momentum threw her to the ground, instinctively I reached out for her but the distance between us prevented me from making contact with her, she landed head first with this sickening crunch. I was convinced she would be seriously injured, I had shouted to Christine to come out of the shop, she was horrified when she saw the extent of the head injury, Christine is a nurse by profession, she called an ambulance immediately, as she tried to do the best she could to make Vivien comfortable, the ambulance arrived and she was taken to Boston Hospital. Christine accompanied Vivien in the ambulance, Kevin, Charlotte and myself followed in the car.

Vivien was treated immediately at the A&E department of Boston Hospital, the resulting x-rays confirmed that there was no major injury. We were all very relieved with that news, the downside was that Vivien looked as if she just stepped into the ring with Mike Tyson. When I explained the nature of the fall to the doctor, he was very surprised that there was no significant injury, he was of the opinion that the fact that Vivien had been on HRT for the past 35 years was the contributory factor to the strength of her bones. I just thought she was naturally boneheaded. Upon her discharge we all drove back to Billinghay. Kevin and Chris loaded up the car with their newly acquired Christmas decorations, made their farewells and then headed off back home to North Wales. For all the wrong reasons it had been a memorable weekend.

36

We received a telephone call from the hospital at Grantham, to be advised that Marlene had been readmitted, and that she was very poorly, and could we please contact Thomas.

Thomas was receiving dialysis at Lincoln Hospital, by the time we got to Grantham Hospital sadly she had passed away. Thomas took it very badly. I arranged the funeral and Marlene was buried in the little church at Cranwell. Thomas had found a really nice cottage in a village called Brant Broughton he was very happy there with his cats.

Vivien was a little bit concerned by the strange sounds that my chest made while I was sleeping. I agreed, under duress, to go and see the GP. For the second time, he recommended that I present myself at a rapid response clinic. I asked him, 'When should I go?' 'Now would be a good time,' he replied. Viv was still at work so I drove over to her workplace, her boss told her to leave and go and to take me to the hospital. The resulting examination confirmed a left-sided pneumothorax.

There were complications when they tried to fit a chest drain, and to reinflate my left lung. I was eventually referred to a thoracic specialist at Nottingham Gen Hospital and he confirmed that I needed a surgical procedure.

I had arranged a surprise birthday party for Viv at the Plough Inn at Walcott. Viv's sister Avril and her husband Dennis had brought Megan with them to come and see what our house was like, now that it was all finished, they were all very impressed. Vivien was even more surprised when Thomas turned up dressed up to the nines saying he was looking forward to his birthday dinner. The night was a great success. Viv took her mum, Avril, and Thomas back to our house in Billinghay. For whatever reason, Thomas decided that he wanted to go home, both of them left the house at the same time, Viv was returning to the pub to collect Dennis and I, as she pulled into the pub car park Thomas was directly behind her; he flashed his lights, gave a quick toot on the horn, and home he went. As we got home, Avril was on the telephone, she told me that about a mile past the pub Thomas had been involved in an accident and that the ambulance had been called. We raced back to the scene just in time to see the ambulance arrive, the car was in a ditch, and they needed a fire crew to release Thomas. I told Viv to go back home and that I would stay with Thomas, his back had been injured so was quite a tricky job getting out of the car. I think they had to cut the doorpost off, eventually he was taken to Lincoln Hospital, by the time he had been seen to and made comfortable it must have been about eight o'clock in the morning, so I called Viv to tell her that he had been admitted and that she could come and pick me up. His back injuries were complicated due to the fact that he needed dialysis every other day, he was eventually transferred to a special orthopaedic wing in the Sheffield General Hospital. He was there for a long time, due to his immobility he developed horrendous pressure sores on his heels this problem was exacerbated by his renal problems.

The planning ombudsman ruled in our favour and ordered the council to repay our costs, a Pyrrhic victory. Vivien was offered a really good job, she was part of the team that was providing round-the-clock care for a very well-to-do elderly lady, Mrs Parker in a very large house in the little village of Scopwick, this involved her working 12 hour days, then 12 hour nights on a rota, there was a full-time cook, a cleaner, a handyman, and the team of carers. The Christmas rota was adjusted to favour the carers who had children at home for Christmas, that meant the three carers who were working over the holiday would get no time off at all. I was invited to stay at Scopwick House for all the time Vivien would be working. I was also invited to the Christmas dinner. I suggested to Vivien's boss that, if she wanted to give the cook Christmas Day and Boxing Day off, I would do the food. She was taken aback. 'There will be at least 12 people for Christmas dinner, that is an awful lot of work,' she said. She was reassured when Vivien told her that we had catered for lots more than that number. Christmas was a success.

I was given a date for the surgery on my chest as it was classed as non-urgent I had about for a five-month wait. The lady that Viv was looking after had a granddaughter that lived in Nottingham and she had very kindly offered Viv the use of her apartment while I was in hospital. Thomas and I were of the opinion that undertaking a new-build now was out of the question, we were going to pool our resources and find a suitable property that we could all live in. I saw a property that was advertised on line that had two bungalows and a swimming pool on the same plot, this this was on the Isle of Sheppey in Kent. We arranged a viewing then Viv and I drove down to Kent. We were very impressed, the smaller bungalow was perfect for Thomas, the second one needed some work doing on it but that's what we do, the house was called, Cliffhanger – it was aptly named, it was at the bottom of an unmade lane at Eastchurch Gap and it was on the edge of a cliff. It was predominantly London clay and it had a history of erosion, I checked with the neighbours, and with some local online searches, and we were satisfied that if the house did fall into the Thames estuary, it wouldn't be in our lifetime. We made an offer, it was accepted and the moving date was agreed.

We had no problem finding a buyer for our house, we were advised sell the plot complete with planning permission at the next property auction, We hired a local house mover to move the bulk of our belongings. Thomas was a passenger in the removal van, Vivien drove her car, and I followed in Thomas's car, both cars were loaded to the gunwales. Thomas was absolutely delighted with his bungalow the views over the Thames estuary were fabulous. The front of our bungalow looked like a Spanish villa, with a very nice decked veranda. We had not been on the Isle of Sheppey very long when it became necessary to familiarise ourselves with the services on offer at Medway Hospital. I needed a trip to the A&E department, they just confirmed that I had a lung problem that needed surgical intervention, these procedures were called a pleurodesis and a pleurectomy, and they said they would arrange an appointment for the surgery. I telephoned my last GP Dr Hinchcliffe from Billinghay for his advice, he said, 'Under no circumstances must you undergo lung surgery at the Hospital in Kent, you must go to Nottingham.' We confirmed that the generous offer of accommodation for Viv in Nottingham from Mrs Parker's granddaughter was still available, as it was a 350 mile round trip. So we turned up the on the appropriate date at the thoracic pulmonary clinic at Nottingham Hospital. During the discussion with the surgeon, just before I went in for the procedure, he advised us, that this was a very serious operation that involved the removal of the diseased lung tissue, and that they were going to peel back the lining of the lung the pleura, sand it down, then stick it back together. They would take biopsies from the lung to check that there was nothing sinister in there. The real good news was that this was a high risk procedure – fortunately, I had never smoked, unfortunately, there have been occasions in the past when I have been in contact with asbestos. The diagnosis was, diffuse pleural thickening. This condition could cause problems during a long-haul flight, so we had to cancel the trip to Australia again. Although the flight looked very dubious it did not dampen my enthusiasm for a trip down under, I could always go by boat.

The procedure went well. I was kept in for about a week. As usual, I was told that there will be no driving for a couple of weeks. I was duly discharged, Viv had to drive so I was a reluctant passenger, just outside Cambridge we encountered a massive thunderstorm, the visibility was that bad we had no choice but to get off the main road, park up and wait for the storm to pass. Then it was onto the M25, over the Dartford Crossing and then onto the Isle of Sheppey. Viv rose to the challenge admirably. We had arranged for a couple of Thomas's friends to come and look after him while we were away – a couple of weeks before we left Lincoln Thomas bought a 4x4 so we could get a wheelchair in the back of it, it developed a problem and as it was still under warranty it had got to go back to the garage in Lincoln. This involved Thomas's friend driving his car back to the garage in Lincoln followed by Viv. Viv, then took her home, then drove back to the Isle of Sheppey on her own, another hell of a day's driving. There was some work to do in our bungalow, we had a new kitchen fitted by a couple of local guys. They made quite a good job of fitting the kitchen, we were impressed with the standard of their workmanship. Because there was no town gas, we had to use LPG, one of the guys who done the kitchen work said he could fit a new boiler and radiators, we made the mistake of paying him £2000 upfront for the materials, big misjudgement by me, we never saw him again. On a more positive note, he did leave all his tools in our house, he never saw them again.

37

Now that all the work was done the house was really comfortable, we were open for visitors. Dennis and Avril were first, they came for a weekend and thoroughly enjoyed themselves. Thomas's bungalow was separated from ours by his decked patio that had a small flight of steps leading down to our patio. The steps were no use to Thomas, we decided to remove the steps and build a ramp, that could facilitate the use of Thomas's wheelchair. Dennis very kindly volunteered his time to help with this project. We sourced all the materials needed then Dennis returned and spent a few days with us to complete it. We were all very pleased with the end result and Thomas could easily come from his bungalow to our bungalow and use the pool of he wanted to.

When I've got nothing to do I tend to get bored very easily, under duress Viv went along with my plan to buy an old motorboat and fix it up as my summer project, the boat and trailer were duly acquired, brought home I started to work on it. It was great fun, this was only a small 16 foot Fletcher motorboat with an outboard engine, it took a few months to get it ready but I was enjoying it. My nephew Thomas came for a visit he was quite impressed with both of the bungalows, the swimming pool and the boat. I was looking to buy a small shed there was one for sale in the village. Tom and I went to look at it, it fitted the bill so I decide to buy it. The seller enquired as to how we were going to move it. Tom said, 'No problem mate it will fit on the roof of my car.' It did, and we very carefully drove home with it tied to his roof rack.

Tom obviously enjoyed his visit with us, because not many weeks after his father, mother and two sisters came for a visit. I think the Isle of Sheppey had turned into the holiday destination for the Jones family. During this visit Kevin and I decided to see if this boat would float. Kevin hitched the trailer to the back of Thomas's car, Viv and the girls followed behind in their car, we went down to the beach at Sheerness. Kevin reversed down the ramp and positioned the boat on the shingle just above the waterline, I released all the securing straps climbed into the boat and gave Kevin the okay to launch. What an anti-climax! It slid halfway off the trailer, then got stuck. I had completely misjudged the state of the tide, the stern was in the water, with the bow somehow pointing skywards, the following waves crashed on, and into the boat. On the upside, because of the sudden increase in the weight of the boat due to the water that I was now knee-deep in, the boat gracefully slid off the trailer and floated – when I use the term floated gracefully, that may be a bit of an exaggeration, we were very close to actually replicating the maiden voyage of the *Titanic* – fortunately the boat was still tethered to the trailer so at least it could not float away. The girls were all standing just beyond the waterline and they were all doing a lousy job of concealing their amusement at the predicament that both Kevin and I found ourselves in trying to empty the water out of the boat. Kevin called his daughter Sarah to come close and take his mobile phone off him and to look after it, she said okay dad and put his phone in her pocket. All four of the girls paddled into the water, two on either side to help stabilise the boat while Kevin and I bailed. Sarah moved from the bow to the midships, when the next big wave came the boat rode the wave with Sarah hanging onto the gunwale. She was suddenly up to her armpits in seawater. The three girls on the bow were just up to the knees in the water and everybody laughed including Kevin and I at Sarah's predicament. We all laughed even more when Sarah asked her dad, 'Is your phone waterproof?' as it was still in her pocket. Kevin was not amused, the tide was still coming in and the big waves were getting very scary. As we got the water out more came in, we decided to abandon the launch and call it a day. Kevin repositioned the trailer, and we commenced the process of hauling the boat out, big mistake, due to the amount of water still in the boat the additional weight buckled the struts on the trailer, we had to wait until the water had run out through the drain hole. As the tide was still making and we were on the shingle, there was a possibility that we could lose the boat, the trailer and the car, fortunately a gentleman with a 4x4 came to our assistance. Using the two vehicles we were able to tow both the car and the trailer onto the concrete slipway and wait patiently for the water to drain out. It was quite obvious to this guy that we were absolute novices when it came to launching a motorboat, he told me about a much quieter safer place where it would be ideal to launch, if we ever tried to do this again, it was not far from the old road bridge. We decided to cut our losses and take the boat back home, when this was done we all went back home, showered and changed and went for nice meal, and the only fish we ate that night is what we actually had to buy in the restaurant and not what we had hoped to catch on our maiden fishing trip. On our way to the restaurant we did check out the site that the guy had recommended for the relaunch, and true to his word it was just like he said, nice and quiet and calm. The following day I was able to borrow a small boat and trailer, we took it down to this new spot and launched it perfectly. The girls were happy to go shopping for the day so they arranged to come back and pick us up in the early evening, at least Kevin did get to do a bit of boat fishing, albeit very unsuccessfully. The following day he was able to do some beach casting and had a couple of bites so at least he did catch a couple of fish.

They thoroughly enjoyed the rest of their holiday, bounding about in the pool and pretending be in some exotic location. On their final evening we had a barbecue on the patio, we invited a couple of the neighbours – our next door neighbour June was an ex-pub landlady, she was absolutely charming, and a lovely old lady, we all got on famously, her next-door neighbour on the other side, were Jenny and Malcolm. They were good neighbours too, after our disaster with the kitchen fitter, one of Malcolm's sons came to do some work for us, he was a good lad. Malcolm and Jenny ran the local gardening club, they became good friends, we all had a really pleasant evening and there was sadness when it was time to go. Kevin and Chris packed the car and set of the following day, thanking us profusely for such a wonderful holiday and we vowed to do it again soon.

After the boat fiasco, Viv put a foot down with a firm hand and she decided that my days of messing about with boats was at an end. I had no choice but to agree, the boat was sold. Now I had to find a new hobby. We decided it was time that we paid a visit to North Wales and see Viv's mum. We arranged for Thomas's friends to come down from Lincoln spend a couple of days with him while we were away. When we were in Ruthin we asked Megan if she wanted to come back to the Isle of Sheppey with us for a holiday, she was very happy to come for a visit. She fell in love with Thomas's bungalow and she was never happier when she could wield a duster or a dish cloth, with its new fitted kitchen and tiled floors throughout it was easy to keep clean and she was overjoyed when Thomas suggested to her that she should move in and become his permanent housekeeper. Megan and I would sit on our front veranda overlooking the river, she really did look the part, resplendent in her white floppy sun hat, sporting my binoculars round her neck, that gave her that jaunty nautical look. She enjoyed a bit of people watching due to the constant stream of holidaymakers going down to the beach. She also made a point of advising me, and describing in great detail the particulars of every ship that sailed past, this was the Thames estuary one of the busiest waterways on the planet, but Megan felt duty bound keep me informed, needless to say I didn't get much reading done. She enjoyed her stay with us and when we took a back home to North Wales, Kevin and Chris told us they would be coming back for a long weekend very shortly.

38

True to their word they turned up couple of weeks later. It was not so hectic this time just a bit of beach fishing and chilling by the pool, while they were here on this trip, we received the disturbing call from North Wales that advised us that Dennis and Avril have been involved in a serious road traffic accident, when the emergency services arrived, the paramedics needed the assistance of the Fire Brigade to free Avril from the car. They had to cut the roof off, the air ambulance was called, and Avril was airlifted to the local hospital, once she had been stabilised she was then transferred to the specialist trauma unit at Liverpool's Royal Infirmary. We travelled back up to North Wales, checked in with Megan then went to visit Dennis at Glan Clwyd hospital – he underwent surgery on his knee and he was on the mend. We then went on to Liverpool to visit Avril, her injuries were more severe, she had surgery on her arm, shoulder, chest and foot, she still limps today. It transpired that the other driver veered across the road on a bend, struck their car and pushed it through the fence and rolled over into a field, they were very lucky. We spent another couple of days in North Wales then we headed back to the Isle of Sheppey.

Viv managed to find herself a part-time job doing a little cleaning work in one of the local pubs called The Halfway House, as per usual, somehow I managed to end up helping out in the kitchen, it started to get busy, and then it was turning out to be a full-time job, this was not what we wanted, so we had to call it a day.

The wounds on Thomas's feet, due to poor circulation were getting worse he was hospitalised a couple of times, I was sufficiently concerned enough to call Val our sister, to tell her she should come over from Ireland. We were able to spend a couple of days with him, it was late afternoon and we were just about to leave as we got to the door he called me back. I leaned over his bed and said to me, 'I love you.' 'As do I, we will see you tomorrow,' was my reply. I was called by the ward sister at about 2 am she told me that Thomas had passed away and that we could come to see him after 10 am. When we arrived the porter took us down to the chapel, as he opened the door to let the girls in he said to me, 'You have my condolences it is always very sad when you lose your father.' I replied, 'Thank you for your kind sentiments but he is my younger brother.'

It was Thomas's wish that he be buried at Cranwell next to Marlene, we saw that his wishes were carried out to the letter. It was a very moving service, my brother-in-law Kevin, and his family, along with several members of Marlene's family all came to pay their respects, we gave him a good send off. It didn't take long for us to realise that these bungalows were far too big for just the two of us – due to the close proximity of the sea, these buildings needed the same maintenance programme as that of a boat. We called the estate agents and put both of the bungalows on the market, there was plenty of interest, we got the odd one or two sightseers, but we ended up getting a good price for both of the bungalows and we were able to sell most of the contents along with all our garden furniture, we even managed to sell Thomas's 4x4. We decided it was time that we would move back to North Wales so that Viv would be closer to her family. We would drive up to Ruthin, spend a few days with Megan, and check out any prospective houses that may fit the bill. We viewed about half a dozen properties, but none of them fitted the bill. We drove back to Sheerness. A couple of days later one of Viv's sisters had sent us a copy of their local rag, there was a house advertised for sale but it was not in the usual estate agents column, this ad had been placed in the items for sale section. This ad was for a two bedroomed detached bungalow. I telephoned the number in the ad, the guy I spoke to gave me the details, and the address. I called Sue to ask her if she wouldn't mind going to have a look at the house, and to give me her opinion.

A couple of days later she called me and said that it was a nice looking property. We called the guy and made an appointment to view the house the following weekend. We drove back up to North Wales. The house was okay, it was in dire need of a complete refit, the garden was enormous, and it had a detached garage. I went and introduced myself to my soon-to-be next door neighbour, John. I wanted to talk to him about the time that Kimmel Bay was flooded in 1990. Susan was living just round the corner from St Asaph Avenue, and her house was one of the many that had been flooded. John had been living in his house 30 years, without any flooding problems.

39

Our offer was accepted, and as it was a cash sale the move was going to happen pretty quickly, as soon as we got back we started the ball rolling for the next move, same old story, rent a van, find a driver, load the van, put belongings in storage, renovate house, move in, settle down, when I say settle down do I really mean it, since 1982 we have moved house sixteen times. We tied up all the loose ends with our buyers, and as it was a cash deal we trusted them enough to let them move in before the deal was completed, and I must admit now with hindsight, that it didn't do any favours for Vivien's nervous disposition, having to sit outside a bank on Rhyl High Street for four hours, waiting and praying that the transfer of funds would be completed before the bank closed. Until it was a done deal we had been staying with Megan. Being there with her made us realise that she was suffering with the onset of dementia. Kevin and a couple of his sisters had a rota system in place that ensured at least one of them would be there to see to Megan's needs during the day.

Once we had moved in it started all over again, knocking walls down, new kitchen, shower room, and a bathroom but this time I had some really good help, my new neighbour Gwen, her son James was a bricklayer, he done all the masonry work and fitted an RSJ, that we conveniently found in the back of the garage. Obviously going to be used by the previous owner. We were also very fortunate to be introduced to Vladimir, the only way to describe him is as a master craftsman, he was literally a jack of all trades, he also had a friend. Stephan who would come and give him a hand if and when it was needed, these two guys were from Bulgaria. We got even more good news from Australia, Corey now had a baby brother called Jem. The work on the house was moving along at a steady pace, the back garden was huge with a small patio, we decided that a decent-sized conservatory, with a timber decked patio would look good.

I started to look around for a conservatory, I found one in St Helens, the factory had just gone into liquidation and they were selling off their assets. The conservatory was in their showroom and we agreed a price, I paid a deposit, and I was told that it would be dismantled and delivered to my home, there I would pay the balance, when it was delivered I was shocked to see a mountain, of frames, panels, brackets, and glazing packs stacked up in my back garden. This was a DIY step too far. When Vladimir arrived I took him out into the back garden to see the mountain. I said to him, 'this might be a big mistake I would not know where to begin.' 'That is absolutely no problem, in Bulgaria Stephan was the manager of a double glazing factory'. Vladimir and Stephan worked together to dig the footings and to lay the concrete slab, Stephan completed the construction of the conservatory on his own, with the occasional bit of help from me.

Viv had found herself a part-time job she really liked, she was a dinner lady at a primary school in Rhyl.

Megan's state of health had deteriorated to such a state it became obvious that she was going to need constant care, and on a couple of occasions she was found wandering around the square in the wee small hours dressed only in a nightgown. The family decided that they needed to find a decent care home, after checking out about maybe half a dozen different establishments, we were amazed at the variation of standards that we found that were considered acceptable – from the overwhelming odour of cabbage, that smelled like it had been boiled for two hours in urine, plus the attitude of some of the so-called carers, we came away with the opinion that some of them would be more than highly qualified enough to run a training course for traffic wardens and estate agents. The girls were fortunate enough to find a care home that was really suitable, it was down on the beach road at Prestatyn. This was a very nice care home, it was spotlessly clean and Megan's room was very nice, and the care staff were brilliant, but it would be remiss of me if I failed to highlight the exceptionally high standard of care that was shown, not only to Megan but also to the rest of the residents. There was one carer in particular to whom we all would be eternally grateful for the outstanding level of care that she provided. Her name was Debbie, she treated Megan as if she was her own mother, but Megan, being Megan, showed no aversion to berating her, as she did her own son, her daughters, and her sons-in-law, long before the Alzheimer's set in.

We received some great news from Australia, the whole family would be coming over to the UK for a visit, they would be going to the Wirral for a few days to see Christopher's mother and family, then down to Brighton to see Sam's friends and family, they would be spending the bulk of their time in North Wales.

We rented a house for them for the duration of their stay. We had a great time getting to meet my two grandsons, we got to spend some quality time with the two boys Corey and Gem. We had rented a minibus in order to pick them up from the airport, Vivien and I had booked an airport hotel for the night as it was an early morning pickup. The drive back to North Wales was uneventful, but there was one minor incident which still causes me to chuckle today – we were driving through the little town of Buckley and we had to stop at a traffic signal. Corey looked out of the window and said to his mother, 'What are these funny little buildings?' We had stopped alongside a row of terraced houses. Time passed far too quickly it was soon time for them to leave, we had arranged to have a barbecue in the garden a couple of days before they left, all of Viv's family came as did my sister Valerie, and one of the daughters Imelda, there were floods of tears and much hugging when we left them at the airport for their flight back home to Australia.

My nephew Thomas had just bought a house just up the road from where we were, we agreed to help them out with the move and to give a hand some of the renovations that were needed, this was an ex-local authority house that came with some restrictions, the only one that caused a problem was that he was not allowed livestock in his garden, he had three chickens. He said, 'Uncle Mike will you look after my chickens please I have a hen house and a fence that you can have.' A couple of days later Kevin and Thomas turned up with the hen house, some wire, and three chickens. Our back garden was huge, so we set about placing the hen house in the bottom corner and fenced it off, the hens didn't look very happy, we decided they needed a bigger pen, needless to say we ended up building a massive chicken coop, it stretched the whole width of the back garden, that is about 36 ft, then an L-shaped section of about 18 ft in length. We bought about another half dozen birds, three were silkies, we kept them in the smaller hen house. Tom's in-laws also donated another hen house with occupants, an associate of Kevin's also donated a hen house, along with a cockerel, his name was Rocky, we were now a fully-fledged chicken farm, things were was getting out of hand as we had over 30 chickens – on the positive side we would often take some of the baby chicks to the care home for the residents to see, they liked them that much that the owner of the care home wanted to know if we could sell him a small hen house and a couple of chickens which they could keep just for the residents. The following day we took one of the hen houses and two chickens to the care home, the residents and the staff were delighted with their gift, unfortunately one neighbour complained about the noise, this was only two chickens, but the manager couldn't risk falling foul of his neighbours.

We took them back home the next day. Rocky was very busy we ended up with about 35 chickens – it was getting out of hand, but the neighbours were all very pleased with their endless supply of fresh eggs. Rocky was very protective of his flock, entering the enclosure without checking where he was very risky, we had a small internal door between both sections, on one occasion I must have left it open, I was in the bottom half of the run cleaning one of the houses when he came thundering through, and when he was running he looked impressive. I just had time to pick up the side panel of the chicken house and hold it in front of me like a shield, he leapt at it burying both his spurs in my legs, crashing against my makeshift shield and straining his neck over the top with his beak about a quarter of an inch away from my eyes. it was scary, I was lucky to get out in one piece. There was another occasion when I was outside of the run and Viv was inside, he started to make his run so I shouted to Viv, 'You need to get out.' She turned to get away and she tripped, as she fell the momentum carried her out of the run and onto her backside in the garden, I had a spade in my hand, the only thing I could think of was, that I must decapitate him, but he came out of the run and just stopped, he looked at Viv lying in the mud, ruffled his feathers, scratched the mud, then went back into the run.

40

Due to my ongoing lung problem, I got involved the British Lung foundation and joined their local Breathe Easy group. One of the members informed me that if you have a lung condition and you are keeping chickens it will have the same effect on you as if you are smoking 30 a day, the chickens have got to go. Reluctantly, we also decided that it was becoming increasingly more difficult to keep the garden tidy – it is just too big, we needed to downsize, maybe find an apartment or very small bungalow without a garden. So we called the estate agent, and here we go again.

We had no difficulty in finding a buyer for our house, with the added bonus that they wanted the entire contents of the garden including furniture, chicken houses, and chickens – it was a win–win situation. The prospective buyers who wanted to buy the house were Steve, Cath and their daughter Katie, to describe them as animal lovers would be a bit of an understatement, they had cats, dogs, rabbits, hamsters, ducks, a couple of canaries, a parakeet, and of course all the chickens that we left.

We viewed a couple of apartments but nothing seemed to fit the bill, they were too small, but we did find a three-bedroom bungalow with a small garden, the house was in need of a full renovation but that didn't faze us so we put in an offer and it was accepted, we thought it would take about three months for completion. We had managed either to sell or rehome most of the chickens, any that were left, the prospective buyers were happy to keep them.

We had developed a rigid cleaning programme for the hen houses – I would get all of the bits and pieces that we needed ready in my shed while Viv cleaned the houses. While I was in the shed I started to feel uneasy. I called out to Viv all I could do was stutter incoherently, I was also slobbering like a rabid dog, Viv was concerned enough to call for an ambulance, and when the paramedics arrived they confirmed that I had had a mini stroke. During my conversation with the paramedics I was able to tell them that in the early hours I was woken from a strange dream that somehow involved large concrete block sitting on my chest, and that my left arm felt so weak I couldn't lift myself out of bed, so I just lay there and must have dropped off again. When we got up we had breakfast and somehow I omitted to tell Viv what had happened during the night, Needless to say I was on the receiving end of a very severe tongue lashing from Viv for not having the good sense to wake her. I was admitted to A&E and subject to a raft of tests that confirmed that I had suffered a TIA they kept me in for 24 hours observation, then I was discharged into the tender loving charge of my dear wife.

We checked the new bungalow over, and confirmed that it was in need of a total refurb. It was time to call Vladimir. I also, always make a point of checking my soon to be new neighbours. Next door on the left, there is Daryl and Katie, a very pleasant young couple. On our right side, there is Wal and Alex, again a very nice young couple.

Eventually when the house sale was completed we were able to move in, and after a couple of days Vladimir and his assistant arrived to start the work.

Cath was very involved with a pet rescue charity, she was also very well known to the local vet, so consequently, she ended up running a sort of animal recuperation service, any cat, dog, or any other four-legged animal as well as anything with feathers, that had been either abandoned or injured. We went back to the house one day to see her for something, and she was nursing a pair of baby seagulls. Unfortunately Vivien's cat Charlotte, had been unwell eventually we had to take it to the vet to be put to sleep.

Viv was very upset she gets very attached to her pets, she decided this time that you would not get another cat.

Christopher and Sam decided that they wanted to come for another visit we thought this was a fabulous idea. They went ahead with their plans and when they confirmed days and dates we were pleased to find out that they had chosen Manchester Airport, we were going to rent another minibus, but my nephew Thomas suggested that we just go in two cars that would be sufficient.

About two weeks before our visitors from down under arrived, Cath turned up at our house with the tiniest kitten I have ever seen, it was a feral cat that had been abandoned. Cath had taken pity on it, she had taken it home with her and it had to be bottle fed every two hours, she was very doubtful that it would survive. Two days later she brought it up to see if Vivien wanted to keep her, she was called Poppy. I said no, but as per usual I was overruled. The kitten was still very fragile and we all were still not a hundred percent sure that it would survive, we had it in a little carry box in the front living room. Viv and I were sitting on the settee, it came out of the box very cautiously sniffing its new surroundings, it came over to the settee, looked at both of us then proceeded to climb up my left leg then on to my stomach and tried to burrow itself into the crook of my elbow, I was the chosen one, I now belonged to the cat.

When we met them at the airport we were amazed how much the boys have grown. As this was a three-bedroom bungalow, although it was a bit cramped, we were able to put them up here with us, they were here for the month, we bought a little runabout for their use, they did their trip to the Wirral. Then down to Brighton to see Sam's mum and friends, they spent the bulk of the time with us here in Towyn, it was really good to get to know the boys now as they were older. Both Corey and Jem had shown a great interest in music, so much so, a couple of years ago for their Christmas presents, we sent them a full-size drum kit, and an electric guitar, during one of our Skype conversations I was very surprised when they both decided to sing and play their favourite song for us, we were half expecting some obscure Justin Bieber track or something similar to that, we were literally blown away when they struck up, 'Wild Thing' by the Troggs. We were very impressed with their taste in music of the 1960s.

As we had literally no garden space we were at odds to being able to provide a farewell barbecue. My cousin Carol came to the rescue, she has a beautiful home in old Colwyn, with breath-taking views overlooking Colwyn Bay, she put her house and garden at our disposal. Carol's son Andrew is a performer, he had managed to bring together about a dozen people from various bands who offered their services for the bash. We bought a marquee so if it rained it didn't matter, we organised all the food and drink, there was going to be about 40 people attending, including some of my other cousins who I hadn't seen for maybe 40 years. Chris, Corey, Jem and myself went up to see Andrew to discuss what was going to happen on the party night. Andrew suggested that Corey and Jem could borrow a couple of guitars and that they should play a few songs at the party. Corey agreed on one condition, that Granddad plays the drums for him. I said to Corey, 'I am so sorry to disappoint you, but I no longer have a drum kit.' Andrew then proceeded to tell me that one of my cousins, Roy Myler was still in a band, and that they were prepared to play as long as I agreed to play drums with them, and not to worry as there will be a drum kit provided, so it looked like I had no choice, not that I was complaining. I was now really looking forward to it. The weather stayed very kind to us, and the party was a storming success, as was the debut performance of the Nolan Trio. The month ended far too soon, we had a fabulous time really getting to know the boys well, it was also very good for me getting reacquainted with my cousins from way back we had a lot to talk about it was great. Andrew has his own production company and they regularly put on murder mystery shows, he suggested that maybe he should put a show on and the proceeds should go to my Breathe Easy group, this sounded like a good idea we found a suitable venue where we could provide a full three course Sunday lunch, Andrew's company would put on their show, and my cousin Roy would be happy to provide the musical entertainment. On the proviso that I played drums with them. We settled for a Valentine's day lunch – the Valentine's day massacre, would be the theme of the murder mystery, and the band will be there to provide further entertainment. The day was a brilliant success, the only downside was Viv and I had greatly underestimated the amount of hard work that went into feeding 40 people, but everybody thought it was brilliant, Viv's two sisters, Iona and Susan, plus Christine, her sister-in-law, along with my cousin Carol were a great help in the kitchen, and the icing on the cake we made about £140 for the Breathe Easy group.

The only external work that we had to do involved replacing fencing panels. This was Kevin's field of expertise. The only downside to this was 'Dougal', an extremely large, playful Labrador that belongs to Wal and Alex, our next door neighbours. Unfortunately, Kevin has a pathological fear of dogs.

Fortunately, Alex was very pregnant, as Alex was admitted to hospital, Dougal went on holiday. Kevin and I were able to do all the fencing without the constant threat of Kevin being eaten by a big dog. Alex was duly discharged, and she brought home a beautiful baby daughter, Eira During a conversation with Wal, it transpired that he was unwell, that is a bit of an understatement, he was battling a very aggressive cancer. I was in awe of the level of fortitude and stoicism that he dealt with his devastating illness. He was in remission, and was looking forward to going back to work and spending some quality time with his new daughter. His illness came back with a vengeance. We would sit in the garden and talk utter rubbish for ages. He asked me if I would mind taking in a few parcels for him over the next couple of days, over 20 parcels arrived for him. Shortly after his readmission to hospital, Alex and Wal were married from his hospital bed. Wal's greatest wish was that he should be allowed to go home and spend his last days with Alex and Eira.

The war was lost on Valentine's day. Alex was devastated, she had lost the love of her life. We went along to the wake, it was very moving. When Alex delivered the eulogy, there was not a dry eye in the room as she paid tribute to Wal. A very large lump came to my throat as she described his legacy to her. He had bought her 25 presents, one for each birthday for the next 25 years.

41

We received an invitation to a 50th wedding anniversary party, it was from a couple that we used to work with at Arbury Hall, Bill and Marjorie Golder. Marjorie and her sister Edie worked together at Arbury Hall during the time we were there, as well as work colleagues they also became very good friends. Marjorie was married to Bill, and they have a daughter Alison. They lived on one of the properties on the Arbury estate, we do keep in touch, birthday cards and Christmas cards supplemented with the odd phone conversations, we were really looking forward to a catch up and a good old natter. The party was to be held at a really nice hotel in Bedworth. We decided, as it was going to be a lunchtime party, we would travel up the day before and overnight there at the hotel, then when it was over we could have had a leisurely drive back home.

I was watching the news on the TV. They were covering yet another dramatic terrorist attack in Belgium, there was an incident on a on a train, and the more severe incident at Brussels airport, it was not until the following day when they started to release the names of the victims that we realised, with absolute horror, that we knew two of the victims. The two youngsters that were killed when none other than Alexander and Sascha Pinczowski. We were not absolutely sure but the names were quite memorable, we checked with our friends in Denmark, and they confirmed, that it was the son and daughter of Ed and Marjan, this was the family that Viv and I worked for when we were living in St Maarten.

Alexander and Sascha were in transit on their journey back to the US, the children were actually on the phone to the parents while they were in line at the American Airlines check-in desk when the suicide bomber detonated his device. Alexander and Sascha were killed instantly they had no chance, both Ed and Marjan were absolutely devastated, as were we, we sent our messages of condolences, but it seemed almost pointless, what can you say?

We made all our plans to head off to this silver wedding celebration. We were not in any hurry so we set off at about two o'clock, just outside Shrewsbury we were approaching a roundabout, we needed to go right so I was in the outside lane, the car in front of me, for no apparent reason, stopped dead, there was a line of moving traffic to my left, and the crash barrier to my right, I couldn't go anywhere. I ran into the back of the car. Vivien had just leaned forward to pick something up from the floor well. I was able to brace myself just before impact Viv was not so lucky, her chest neck and shoulder were badly bruised. I got out of the car, there was a couple in the car in front, the driver got out of his car, I asked him why he stopped suddenly he just mumbled something about traffic lights, we exchanged details and he drove off. Viv was struggling with her breathing, I had to call 999, the police traffic officer was there very quickly, he was able to give the ambulance driver all the particulars and location. This was a very busy road we needed to get off this main road soon as it was safe enough to move. The police officer instructed me to drive to the roundabout and take first left there would be a layby so you can pull in there. The police officer stopped the traffic we were able to get off the main road we were safely tucked in the layby when the ambulance arrived. The paramedics took Viv into the ambulance to check her over and the police officer joined me in the car to take my statement. The officer was of the opinion that we had just become the victims of a crash for cash scam. Things continued to go downhill, my breakdown recovery plan did not cover accidental damage, somehow I had also gotten my car insurance companies contact information mixed up with my household insurance, when the policeman called the insurance company all that he got was a recorded message saying that the office was closed, call again in the morning. The car was just about drivable so he suggested that we check into a hotel that was quite close by. Viv was given a clean bill of health by the paramedics, and on her insistence they checked me out. I was okay. The traffic officers escorted us to the nearby hotel where we checked in, needless to say they only had one room left, at some ridiculous nightly rate, we had no choice. There was no restaurant facility at this hotel, fortunately there was a decent pub within walking distance, we had a basic meal went back to the hotel and turned in. Just when I thought things couldn't get any worse, when I eventually got through to the insurance company, I was told that the only policy that I held with them was for my household insurance, and not a motor policy. I did not have a car insurance policy with this company. As I constantly change the insurers of my car, I could not remember who I was insured with, as you can imagine Viv was not best pleased when she heard, 'You don't have insurance.' The only option left open to me was to flick through the Yellow Pages alphabetically, I got as far as the RAC before I could find out exactly who I was insured with, the bad news was, it was going to take them another full day to sort things out. We made the call to Viv's brother Kevin, his daughter Charlotte said 'I'll come and get you now see, you in about an hour and a half.'

We arranged with the reception at the hotel that the car was recovered as soon as possible, it was up to the insurance company now. I had called our friends in Warwickshire to apprise them of the situation and offered our regrets for not being able to attend the party. The insurance company decided that the car was a write-off, so we had to find another car.

Viv had a big birthday coming up, she didn't want any fuss just a low-key event as she put it, as it transpired we ended up renting the back room of the Morton Arms, with the pub catering for about 40 guests, the party was a great success.

It was my turn next, having a similar birthday in December, we were going to repeat the booking at the Morton. My nephew Andrew offered to put on a show, as it was during the closed season, we got a good deal hiring the concert room at the Magpie and Stump, they provided a hot buffet, and a full bar service. Andrew's company put on a Jack the Ripper murder mystery, and the music was provided by my cousin Roy's band, with me playing drums. Our friends Debbie and Gary made the journey up from Essex, along with Nick and Chris who had made the journey up from Dorset, and as Nick used to be the vocalist in the band from Okehampton, we got him to sing a few songs. It is safe to assume a good time was had by one and all.

Christmas came and went, things were ticking over nicely. I have one or two medical issues that require constant medication, Vivien administers my pills with military precision, various pills at different times of the day, with my final dose at bedtime. This one particular night I had swallowed the contents of the little plastic cup that had been left out for me, then I went to bed, about half an hour later Viv came into the bedroom and she asked me, 'Where are the pills?' 'I've taken them,' was my reply. 'Oh dear, you have taken one of mine by mistake, what are you going to do?' My reply was 'I am going back to sleep.' 'You can't go to sleep now, I'm going to have to call the out-of-hours NHS.' The resulting telephone conversation necessitated a visit from a couple of paramedics in their ambulance. I was advised that it would be prudent for them to take me to A&E for the night so I could be checked over. There was an issue with my heart rate. Viv followed the ambulance to the A&E department. When I was transferred to a ward, Viv made sure that I was tucked in and as comfortable as possible, when she was satisfied that I was OK she said, 'Goodnight I will see you later.' It was about 4.30 am, then she left me to go back home. I was discharged the following day, after successfully passing an Alzheimer's test.

A couple of weeks later I picked up a chest infection, after three or four visits to the GP, and a cocktail of steroids and antibiotics, my breathing was getting very laboured, once again Viv called the out-of-hours NHS service. She described my symptoms. The operator advised her that the doctor would call her back within the next hour. He did. He asked to talk to me. He told me that he would be around to see me as soon as possible, he was here in less than half an hour, he listened to my chest and he said, 'That sounds like an awful lot of crap in there you need to be in hospital.' He then called for an ambulance, there were a couple of issues that took them just about a week to get sorted before I was able to be discharged. Once again I am in awe of the standards of excellence and professionalism of all the care staff. As I get older, I find myself having to call on their services far more frequently than I would really like to.

42

It was always part of our longer-term plan that we should retire to a nice apartment preferably with a sea view, with this in mind and after the recent health scare we decided that the time was right to look for a new apartment, obviously we needed something with no outside space, and absolute zero maintenance.

After about half a dozen or so viewings we came to the conclusion that, unless Camelot provided the funds, the type of apartment we wanted was way out of our reach. The transition from a three-bedroom detached bunga-low, to a tiny two-bedroom apartment would be totally unrealistic, so after plenty of soul searching we arrived at the executive decision, that this bun-galow would be our forever home. This was not a hard decision to make, we are very happy with this house, plus Vivien's brother Kevin, and two of her sisters live within walking distance.

We have decided to have the all of the drive completely resurfaced with a modern resin coated decorative gravel. We have also decided that the entire patio area at the back of house will be covered as well, this will do away with the need for the annual pressure washing, and perpetual weeding between the patio slabs. We had a couple of quotes, some quite laughable, we settled on a local company from Kimmel Bay that offered a good price along with a ten year guarantee on all work they do, we are looking forward to it all being finished.

A couple of weeks before they were due to start the work, I was sitting at my computer when I very suddenly felt as if my tongue was swelling, it is a startling experience when I had difficulty in breathing through my mouth. I could breathe okay through my nose it just felt very odd. As if on cue, Vivien came into the sitting room with my afternoon medication and a bottle of water. I took the bottle from her, took a mouthful and I found that I couldn't swallow it. I got up, made it to the kitchen sink and spat it out, because of an old injury to my neck I do have an issue trying to swallow if I am drinking from a bottle with my head back. Viv gave me a cup of water. I took a large swallow from it, the water, came out through my nose, my tongue felt that thick I couldn't talk. Viv did not hesitate, she called for an ambulance and told the operator that she was convinced that I was having a stroke, the paramedics arrived very quickly. I felt a bit more comfortable due to the fact that I could breathe without any problem through my nose. The male paramedic was of the opinion that I was having some sort of allergic reaction, the female paramedic confirmed Viv's opinion that I was having a stroke and that I needed to be hospitalised as soon as possible.

While we were en route to the hospital the female crew member called the A&E department to alert the stroke team. When the ambulance arrived I was taken straight in and I was seen by the doctor within half an hour, he confirmed the diagnosis that I was having a stroke. I was taken for a CT scan, and it was confirmed. The scan showed that there was blood clot on my brain. Due to their rapid intervention, they were able to treat me with thrombolytic drugs and remove the clot, I was then transferred to the stroke unit. My main problem, was swallowing, and speech. Due to the possibility of aspiration, all liquids had to be thickened, it was quite traumatic when the reality of the situation reveals that you can't speak, and that you need to be fed gloop with a spoon that was masquerading as water. Thankfully, it only lasted for a couple of days, this was entirely due to the superlative efforts of the dieticians, and speech therapists, once again I am greatly indebted to the healthcare professionals that I had the good fortune to be in the care of. During my stay on the stroke ward – I was there for one week – I witnessed some patients with very severe, speech and mobility problems, once again I realised, just how lucky I had been. During my stay in the hospital I was examined by a thoracic surgeon, this was just to make sure that nothing had gotten into my lungs. The surgeon commented on my collection of scars, and he asked me would I mind donating my body for trainee consultants to use to help with their diagnostic skills. I agreed instantly, on the condition that they give it back to me when they have finished their examination. I had a constant stream of visitors and well-wishers, as well as many, many, get well cards.

Our friends from Dorset, Nick and Chris decided to drive up for a visit, on the day that they planned to arrive we had booked tickets for a concert at Rhyl Pavilion to see the Illegal Eagles, fortunately we were able to secure two additional tickets, so Nick and Chris were able to accompany us to the concert, we all had a great night. The following day Nick and Chris came round for lunch, they gave me a couple of get well cards from the family including a letter from Lee, their son. Last year for my 70th birthday, Lee had promised me a birthday present, due to some logistical problems, the birthday gift did not materialise. Lee apologised and told me it was all in hand, Nick and Chris brought the gift with them, it was well worth the wait, somehow he had managed to get Roger Taylor to personally sign a drum skin, and it was presented to me, along with a Ludwig shoulder bag. Wow! that was some birthday gift, and in the letter accompanying these gifts he made some very touching remarks relating to the time that both my brother Thomas and I had spent with him during his formative early years as an up and coming drummer.

Our granddaughter, Hannah, presented us with our first great grandchild, his name is Solomon, Solly for short. Hannah and Joel live in Perth, so Christopher, Sam and the boys have been very busy flying between Brisbane and Perth for the past few months getting to know the latest addition to the family.

Christopher, Corey and Jem would be coming over here for a visit on 2nd July we are really looking forward to this opportunity of spending some quality time together, Not long after being returned to protective custody, Viv made sure that I would make an almost miraculous recovery. Legally I was not permitted to drive for the next six weeks, if Viv had her way, that would have equated to house arrest, so needless to say I'm very happy to be firing on all cylinders, with only the odd misfire now and again.

This thing we call life is indeed very strange, when faced with adversity, there is often a very positive outcome. I received an email from my sister Val in Ireland, wishing me a speedy recovery and enquiring about my wellbeing, she then went on to tell me that my youngest son, Matthew, had called her after he had heard that I had been in hospital. He asked her if she would pass on his good wishes, and asked her if she thought it would be all right for him to contact me. I have seen Matthew once in 38 years. He called about a week later and said he'd like to come and meet us. Matthew, his wife Sally and Connie, their eldest daughter came over for a visit, it was an experience we all enjoyed, both Viv and I were very surprised to learn that we have just inherited five grandchildren, and there was an additional bonus, one of my grandson's partners is expecting, so we will become great grandparent for a second times. That's quite a lot to take in, but we are working on it. Matthew has three children from his first marriage, Jasmine, his eldest daughter, is currently living and working in the United States. His two sons, twins, Calum, and Oliver, are 18 years of age and they live in Oxford. Matthew and Sally, have two daughters, Connie and Imogen, Connie is 12, and Imogen is 3, going on 30.

Matthew and Christopher are trying to organise a get-together for all of the family during their visit from Australia, this we are really looking forward to. Due to her work commitments, and her new grandchild Solly, Sam will not be able to make the trip with Christopher and the boys this time, and as Jasmine had flown back to the UK three weeks ago for her brothers 18th birthday party, it will be extremely unlikely that she will be able to make it back to the UK for this get-together. If we do not get the chance to meet Jasmine this time, it will be something else we can look forward to in the near future. Christopher and the boys were scheduled to arrive at terminal two at Manchester airport, their flight arrival time was at 0650 hrs on Monday morning, due to the early landing time, and the possibility of heavy traffic we decided to drive to Manchester on the Sunday afternoon, and check into a hotel quite close to the airport for the early arrival on the Monday morning. the hotel we found seemed okay and they even provided a free shuttle bus service to the airport. Matthew called and told us that he would be dropping somebody off at Manchester Airport early Sunday evening, so we gave him the name of the hotel that we had booked and arranged to meet up for supper. Our caution was rewarded, the traffic was horrendous, it took almost two and three-quarter hours to get to Manchester, the journey should have taken one hour 20. We found the hotel and checked in, we were told there was a £10 surcharge for the car parking, that did not go down too well. Matthew arrived almost at the same time as us, he told us that he had to collect somebody else from the airport at 2015, so we ordered him a sandwich and a coffee, and we ordered a couple of bar meals. Vivien told the waiter that she would appreciate it if a sandwich and coffee could be brought immediately, this they did. We had a good chat with Matthew about the arrangements for the following week and he confirmed that his two sons, Callum and Oliver would be coming up from Oxford at the weekend, so we will finally get to meet our two new grandsons. Matthew finished this sandwich and the time came for him to leave, we said our farewells and that we were looking forward to meeting all the family next week. Our food still had not arrived when he left, Vivien called the waiter, he apologised and said the kitchen was busy, eventually the food arrived, definitely not worth the wait. The hotel looked like it had been an old mansion house in the past, it had lots of stairs, corridors, and doors, it took us a wee while to relocate our room, when we eventually found the room, it turned out to be very small, very hot, with a broken air conditioning unit, and windows that didn't open fully. Vivien got no sleep at all, it was that uncomfortable, we were very glad to leave. The original plan was to take the shuttle bus to the airport, pick up Christopher and the boys then return to the hotel for breakfast, we didn't think that this was such a good idea, so when we arrived back at the hotel we took their bags straight out of the shuttle bus and into our car, while Viv went to the desk to check out, and then we left.

43

We had rented a mobile home the duration of their stay that was only a ten minute walk away from our home. We dropped them and their bags off, then while they were freshening up Viv and I went home to prepared a hearty breakfast for them. After they had been fed they went back to the mobile home for a short nap, they returned a couple of hours later and their holiday began.

Christopher and the boys had provided us with a wish list of things they wanted to do, and various types of food and drink they wanted while they were here. The activities ranged from climbing a mountain – well it was just a big hill really – go-kart racing, trout fishing, eating freshly grilled mackerel, with pancakes and bacon, and there was also a competition to see who could eat the most chocolate. Jem's task was to teach Nain how to make Rocky Road, and last but not least Corey had a golf project that needed my help,

For the mountain (hill) climb we were very fortunate to secure the services of professionally trained athlete, Tom Jones, no, not the singing model – 'He is Welsh though' – the micro-brewing model, not only did he provide an excellent barbecued lunch, Christopher very eagerly volunteered his exceptional, and wide ranging, beer tasting experience to Tom, so that he may offer a professional opinion on the quality of the various brews that Tom had available. It was also nice for Corey and Jem to meet up with their Welsh cousins, Daisy and Tobi.

Christopher and the boys went over to the Wirral to meet the rest of their family, his brother Craig had organised a surprise pre-50th birthday party, they all had a good time. Matthew's two sons, Callum and Oliver, had made the trip up from Oxford to complete the family reunion, when Christopher and the boys returned to Towyn, Matthew, Sally, Connie, Imogen, Callum and Oliver came with them. It was a very memorable occasion when Viv and I sat down with Christopher, Matthew, Sally, Corey, Jem, and our newly inherited four grandchildren. The girls went off to the beach, while the guys watched the football, then we all had supper in the bar, Charlotte our niece and Kieron her boyfriend, came over to club to join in and get to know their new cousins, it was a perfect end of a perfect day, and between all that, the family reunions, which included all the Welsh, English, and Australian family members, I think it is safe to assume that a good time was had by one and all. Vivien and I certainly enjoyed it. All we have to do now is to get re-acquainted with our new family, and that will be a whole new story…

Lightning Source UK Ltd.
Milton Keynes UK
UKHW020702270620
365588UK00006B/115